GEORGIA TECH

DAILY DEVOTIONS FOR DIE-HARD FANS

YELLOW JACKETS

Daily Devotions for Die-Hard Fans: Georgia Tech Yellow Jackets
© 2009 Ed McMinn

Library of Congress Cataloging-in-Publication Data
13 ISBN Digit ISBN: 978-0-9801749-5-3

Manufactured in the United States of America.

For bulk purchases or to request the author for speaking engagements, email contact@extrapointpublishers.com.

Go to http://www.die-hardfans.com for information about other titles in the series.

Cover and interior design by Slynn McMinn
Edited by Jean Knight.

YELLOW JACKETS

To Dale Russell,
who makes Tech proud

IN THE BEGINNING

Read Genesis 1, 2:1-3.

"God saw all that he had made, and it was very good" (v. 1:31).

In the beginning, football at Georgia Tech was virtually ignored with "no gate, no crowds, [and] little interest."

As football fever spread across college campuses in the 1890s, a group of students would organize a team and challenge a team from another school or across town. The team usually had little or no official backing from the institution it represented. Football began at Tech in this way in 1892.

Georgia and Auburn christened football in the state with a game at Brisbine Park in Atlanta on Feb. 20, 1892. While local newspapers ignored the event, some Tech students noticed, and on Nov. 5 Tech's first informal team played Mercer. Professor E.E. West served as the volunteer, unpaid coach. The Blacksmiths lost 12-6 and went on to finish 0-3 in that first season, losing 20-10 to Vanderbilt and 26-0 to Auburn.

For eleven largely ignored seasons, football on The Flats limped along with students forming informal teams to play an informal schedule and professors, students, and Atlantans interested in the game volunteering as coaches. The most famous coach in those early days was Lt. Leonard Wood, surgeon general at Fort McPherson. In 1893, he decided to enroll as an undergraduate despite already having a medical degree from Harvard and joined Tech's one-year-old, winless football team as a player-coach. He generally is credited with being the father of Georgia Tech football, its first captain, and in reality its first coach. "Through his zeal . . . the seeds of the rich Ramblin' Wreck tradition were planted," wrote Al Thomy.

Beginnings are important, but what we make of them is even more important. Consider, for example, how far the Georgia Tech football program has come since that first season. Every morning, you get a gift from God: a new beginning. God hands to you as an expression of divine love a new day full of promise and the chance to right the wrongs in your life. You can use the day to pay a debt, start a new relationship, replace a burned-out light bulb, tell your family you love them, chase a dream, solve a nagging problem . . . or not.

God simply provides the gift. How you use it is up to you. People often talk wistfully about starting over or making a new beginning. God gives you the chance with the dawning of every new day. You have the chance today to make things right – and that includes your relationship with God.

The most important key to achieving great success is to decide upon your goal and launch, get started, take action, move.
-- *John Wooden*

Every day is not just a dawn; it is a precious chance to start over or begin anew.

DAY 2

THE WINNING FORMULA

Read 1 John 1:5-10.

"If we confess our sins, he is faithful and just and will forgive us our sins and purify us from all unrighteousness" (v. 9).

Simply put, Bobby Dodd is a legend.

The winningest football coach in Georgia Tech history, Dodd is a member of the College Football Hall of Fame as a player and a coach. He coached at Tech from 1945-1966, compiling a record of 165-64-8 that included two SEC championships and the 1952 national championship. Bear Bryant called Dodd the best game coach he'd ever known. Kim King, the starting quarterback on Dodd's last team and the color analyst on Tech radio broadcasts for more than thirty years, said Dodd was the smartest coach he'd ever known.

So what was Dodd's formula for so much success? He had one, all right – and in the eyes of the old timers, he was a heretic. Dodd believed that college football should be fun. He "discarded all the old rules of sweat and toil and heavy work" and ran relaxed practices that were short, often including a game of touch football. The Jackets rarely hit during the week and frequently played volleyball on Friday.

To the old guard's chagrin, Dodd quite openly fessed up to his unorthodox approach. "I want my players to enjoy the game," he said. His basic guideline was a simple one: He "used methods that he would have wanted his son exposed to." The only training rules he absolutely insisted on were that his players apply themselves to their studies and go to church every Sunday.

Using the simple formula of making the game fun, Dodd built Tech into a national powerhouse in the 1950s.

Perhaps the simple life in America was doomed by the arrival of the programmable VCR. Since then, we've been on an inevitably downward spiral into ever more complicated lives. Even windshield wipers have different settings now.

But you might do well in your own life to mimic Bobby Dodd's very basic approach to football. That is, you should approach your life with the keen awareness that success requires simplicity, a sticking to the basics: Revere God, love your family, honor your country, do your best.

Theologians may make what God did in Jesus as complicated as quantum mechanics and the infield fly rule, but God kept it simple for you: believe, trust, and obey. Believe in Jesus as the Son of God, trust that through him God makes possible your deliverance from your sins into Heaven, and obey God in the way he wants you to live.

That's the true winning formula.

I think God made it simple. Just accept Him and believe.
-- *Bobby Bowden*

**Life continues to get ever more complicated,
but God made it simple for us
when he showed up as Jesus.**

GREAT EXPECTATIONS

Read John 1:43-51.

*"'Nazareth! Can anything good come from there?'
Nathanael asked" (v. 46).*

Good thing they didn't live down to everybody's expectations. Instead, they put together the greatest season in Tech basketball history.

Most publications predicted that the Yellow Jackets of 2003-04 would finish no better than seventh in the ACC. So what happened? Under Coach Paul Hewitt, the ACC Coach of the Year, the Jackets tied the school record for wins and made it to the national championship game for the first time ever.

The key to the season was the continuous growth of the players. B.J. Elder, Isma'il Muhammad, Theodis Tarver, Clarence Moore, Marvin Lewis, Will Bynum, point guard Jarrett Jack, center Luke Schenscher – they all developed as the long season progressed.

In the NCAA Tournament, Elder hit a jumper with 1:06 left to seal the 65-60 win over Northern Iowa that began the run to the championship game. Jack then came up with a big steal in the final six seconds as the Jackets advanced to the Sweet 16 by beating Boston College 57-54.

When Elder, the leading scorer, was injured early on, Lewis stepped up to score 23 points in a 72-67 win over Nevada. In the regional final against traditional powerhouse Kansas, Bynum's three-pointer broke a 71-71 tie and sent Tech on to a 79-71 overtime win and the Final Four.

Bynum drove to the basket around a Schenscher screen for a layup with 1.5 seconds left to propel Tech past Oklahoma State 67-65 and into the championship game where the spectacular run ended with a loss to Connecticut. The team that had no expectations finished with a 28-10 record.

The blind date your friend promised would look like Brad Pitt or Jennifer Aniston but resembled a Munster. Your vacation that went downhill after the lost luggage. Often your expectations are raised only to be dashed. Sometimes it's best not to get your hopes up; then at least you have the possibility of being surprised.

Worst of all, perhaps, is when you realize that you are the one not meeting others' expectations. The fact is, though, that you aren't here to live up to what others think of you. Jesus didn't; in part, that's why they killed him. But he did meet God's expectations for his life, which was all that really mattered.

Because God's kingdom is so great, God really does have great expectations for any who would presume to enter, and you should not take them lightly. What the world expects from you is of no importance; what God expects from you is paramount.

Other people may not have had high expectations for me, but I had high expectations for myself.

-- *Gymnast Shannon Miller*

You have little if anything to gain from meeting the world's expectations of you; you have all of eternity to gain from meeting God's.

DAY 4

UPON MY WORD

Read Matthew 12:33-37.

*"For out of the overflow of the heart the mouth speaks.
The good man brings good things out of the good stored
up in him, and the evil man brings evil things out of the
evil stored up in him" (vv. 34b-35).*

Bobby Ross decided it was time for a talk, and when everything was said, Tech was on its way to a national championship.

After the 0-3 start to the 1989 season, Tech under Ross had lost 16 straight ACC games. Guard Jim Lavin spoke for many of the players when he said, "We're not that good and maybe we never will be. Maybe we're not meant to win."

On the Monday following the third loss, Ross ordered his team to the meeting room. Brandishing lists of players who had missed classes, weight lifting, and workouts, Ross told them he had had enough. "Now you sit in here and hash it out and decide what you want to do," he thundered. Then he delivered the bombshell: If they weren't willing to do it his way and pay the price to win, "then let me know and I'm gonna leave." Ross later said, "I was dead serious" about resigning that day.

The players took over and did indeed hash it out. Senior nose-guard Jeff Mathis spoke of his disgust over the lack of commitment by the players. Lavin said that Mathis told his teammates "the problem was right here in this room." He asked for a show of hands, and the majority wanted to push ahead with Ross and his staff. Nose guard Kevin Battle said, "From that moment on, there was a new commitment. . . . That moment was the turnaround."

A good honest talk turned the Tech football program around and headed it toward the glorious 1990 season.

These days, everybody's got something to say and likely as not a place to say it. Talk radio, 24-hour sports and news TV channels, *Oprah, The View*. Talk has really become cheap.

But words still have power, and that includes not just those of the talking heads, hucksters, and pundits on television, but yours also. Your words are perhaps the most powerful force you possess for good or for bad. The words you speak today can belittle, wound, humiliate, and destroy. They can also inspire, heal, protect, and create. Your words both shape and define you. They also reveal to the world the depth of your faith.

Don't ever make the mistake of underestimating the power of the spoken word. After all, speaking the Word was the only means Jesus had to get his message across – and look what he managed to do.

Watch what you say because others sure will.

My daddy always taught me these words: care and share.
– Tiger Woods

Choose your words carefully; they are the most
powerful force you have for good or for bad.

DAY 5

TEARS IN HEAVEN

Read Revelation 21:1-8.

"[God] will wipe every tear from their eyes. There will be
no more death or mourning or crying or pain" (v. 4).

Yes, there are tears in football – and the emotions of a bunch
of blubbering football players contributed to the snapping of the
second-longest win streak in Georgia Tech football history.

Starting with a 7-0 win over Georgia in the 1914 season, John
Heisman's Golden Tornado teams went 33 games without a loss.
A bunch of Bobby Dodd's Yellow Jackets threatened that streak in
the 1950s. Tech won the last two games of the 1950 season, went
11-0-1 in 1951 and 12-0-0 in 1952, and was 4-0-1 in 1953 when the
Jackets played top-ranked Notre Dame in South Bend, a stretch of
31 games without a loss.

Two factors contributed significantly to Tech's 27-14 loss. First,
Quarterback Pepper Rodgers got hurt on the opening kickoff and
didn't return. Still, Notre Dame led only 7-0 at halftime when the
second factor came into play.

During the break, Notre Dame head coach Frank Leahy had
collapsed and was rushed to the hospital. Freshman Wade
Mitchell, who took over at quarterback after Rodgers and number-
two signal caller Bill Brigman went down, recalled that at Notre
Dame, the teams share a common tunnel, so he was facing the
field when he heard the sound of the Notre Dame team coming
up behind the Yellow Jackets. "I heard all this snorting and nose-

blowing," Mitchell said. "I turn around and they're all bawling, crying like babies. I thought to myself, 'Oh, heck, it is going to be a tough second half.' . . . There was no holding them back." Mitchell was right.

When your parents died. When a friend told you she was divorcing. When you broke your collarbone. When you watch a sad movie.

You cry. Crying is as much a part of life as are breathing and eating. Usually our tears are brought on by pain, disappointment, or sorrow.

But what about when your child was born? When Tech beats Georgia? When you discovered Jesus Christ? Those times elicit tears too; we cry at the times of our greatest, most overwhelming joy.

Thus, while there will be tears in Heaven, they will only be tears of sheer, unmitigated, undiluted joy. The greatest joy possible, a joy beyond our imagining, must occur when we finally see Christ. If we shed tears when Georgia Tech wins a game, can we really believe that we will stand dry-eyed and calm in the presence of Jesus?

What we will not shed in Heaven are tears of sorrow and pain.

If I cry, it means I'm too weak to compete in this sport. That's bull.
-- NASCAR driver Shawna Robinson

Tears in Heaven will be like everything else there:
a part of the joy we will experience.

DAY 6

EXCUSES, EXCUSES

Read Luke 9:57-62.

"Another said, 'I will follow you, Lord; but first let me go back and say good-by to my family'" (v. 61).

If ever a volleyball team could be excused for losing a match, Georgia Tech's 1995 team would have been it.

The Jackets were facing a crucial match with North Carolina on Saturday, Sept. 23. On the line were Tech's home-court win streak (20) and the team's No. 22 national ranking. Shortly before the match, some devastating news shattered the team's focus and left Coach Shelton Collier considering a forfeit.

A late afternoon car wreck had injured team members Andrea Nachtrieb and Jennifer Orr. Jennifer Matullo and other team members were eating their pregame meal when they heard the news, and they rushed to the scene. "It looked awful," Matullo said. "Andrea [Nachtrieb] was out of the car, but Jennifer [Orr] was trapped inside. She was bleeding and crying and really upset." Both girls were taken to Grady Hospital with Orr the more seriously injured, suffering bruises and a broken collarbone.

So as the team suited for the game, Collier looked around and saw distraught, defeated players. He decided against forfeiting, telling his team Nachtrieb and Orr were being taken care of and they had to turn their thoughts to the match. "The minute it's over, we can rush to a phone," he said. Thrust by Nachtrieb's injury into a starting role, Matullo thought, "We have to find a way, and we have to win."

Incredibly, they did, whipping North Carolina 3-1. The team that made no excuses went 29-7, won Tech's second straight ACC championship, and advanced to the second round of the NCAA tournament.

Has some of your most creative thinking involved reasons for not going in to work? Have you discovered that an unintended benefit of computers is that you can always blame them for the destruction of all your hard work? Don't you manage to stammer or stutter some justification when a state trooper pulls you over? We're usually pretty good at making excuses to cover our failures or to get out of something we don't particularly want to do.

That holds true for our faith life also. The Bible is too hard to understand so I won't read it; the weather's too pretty to be shut up in church; praying in public is embarrassing and I'm not very good at it anyway. The plain truth is, though, that whatever excuses we make for not following Jesus wholeheartedly are not good enough.

Jesus made no excuses to avoid dying for us; we should offer none to avoid living for him.

There are a thousand reasons for failure but not a single excuse.
-- Former NFL player Mike Reid

Try though we might, no excuses can justify our failure to follow Jesus wholeheartedly.

THE SUB

Read Galatians 3:10-14.

"Christ redeemed us from the curse of the law by becoming a curse for us" (v. 13).

For one glorious night, junior Jim Stevens was the greatest sub in Georgia Tech football history, leading the Jackets to one of their most exciting bowl victories ever.

In 1972 in his first season as Tech's head coach, Bill Fulcher suspended star quarterback Eddie McAshan the week of the Georgia game, leaving the team in Stevens' little-used hands. Thus the shorthanded 6-4-1 Jackets were underdogs to Iowa State in the Liberty Bowl on Dec. 18.

Iowa State promptly scored twice in the first quarter while Stevens and the Yellow Jacket offense managed minus six yards. But as Fulcher later said about Stevens, "He just got better as the game progressed." In the second quarter, Tech took a 17-14 lead when Stevens tossed a nine-yard touchdown pass to Jim Robinson and Gary Faulkner returned an interception 19 yards for a score.

In the third quarter, Stevens hit Rob Healy for a 22-yard score that sent the teams into the last period tied at 24. Then with less than 12 minutes to play, Stevens completed his incredible game with his third touchdown pass, this one covering three yards to Kevin McNamara. When Iowa State scored and failed on a two-point attempt, Tech had a pulsating 31-30 bowl win.

"It was just fantastic, fantastic," Stevens said in the dressing room after the game. "Didn't Jim Stevens do great?" Fulcher exulted. For the night, Tech's super sub completed 12 of 15 passes for 157 yards and three touchdowns and ran for a two-point conversion. Stevens was named the game's Most Valuable Player.

Wouldn't it be cool if you had a substitute like Jim Stevens for all life's hard stuff? Telling of a death in the family? Call in your sub. Breaking up with your boyfriend? Job interview? Chemistry test? Crucial presentation at work? Let the sub handle it.

We do have such a substitute, but not for the matters of life. Instead, Jesus is our substitute for matters of life and death. Since Jesus has already made it, we don't have to make the sacrifice God demands for forgiveness and salvation.

One of the ironies of our age is that many people desperately grope for a substitute for Jesus. Mysticism, human philosophies such as Scientology, false religions such as Hinduism and Islam, cults, New Age approaches that preach happiness without responsibility or accountability – they and others like them are all pitiful, inadequate substitutes for Jesus.

Accept no substitutes. It's Jesus or nothing.

I never substitute just to substitute. The only way a guy gets off the floor is if he dies.
— *Former basketball coach Abe Lemons*

There is no substitute for Jesus, the consummate substitute.

DAY 8

HOW WE LEAVE

Read 2 Kings 2:1-12.

"A chariot of fire and horses of fire appeared and separated the two of them, and Elijah went up to heaven in a whirl-wind" (v. 11).

We can't always choose how we leave. John Heisman's exit from Tech is a good example.

Heisman arrived on The Flats in 1904 as Georgia Tech's first full-time, paid football coach. He coached at the Institute from 1904 through 1919 with a 102-29-7 record that included four undefeated teams and the 1917 national champions. Heisman was an eccentric, who in addition to being a pioneering coach was a professional actor and a lawyer. Atlanta's many theaters were what lured him to Tech from Clemson, which offered few chances for stage performances. His last drama at Tech was his exit, and a divorce was the cause.

Heisman invited the athletic board members to his house for Sunday lunch, after which he stood up and heaved a bombshell into the room. He told the board, "Mrs. Heisman and I have agreed to separate." After the surprised and somewhat nettled board members had participated in equitably distributing the couple's assets, Heisman delivered yet another surprise: "Because of the difficulties, it has been decided we should not live in the same community. Mrs. Heisman prefers to remain in Atlanta."

Thus, as part of the divorce settlement, Mrs. Heisman got

Atlanta and Tech got its coach's resignation. Al Thomy wrote, "'Embarrassed and flabbergasted' at the turn of events, . . . the board had no choice except to accept the resignation, wish the Heismans well, and announce the news to the press."

John Heisman's leaving Tech ultimately was a decision not entirely of his own making.

You probably haven't always chosen the moves you've made in your life. Perhaps your company transferred you. A landlord didn't renew your lease. An elderly parent needed your care.

Sometimes the only choice we have about leaving is the manner in which we go, whether we depart with style and grace or not. Our exit from life is the same way. Unless we usurp God's authority over life and death, we can't choose how we die, just how we handle it. Perhaps the most frustrating aspect of dying is that we have at most very little control over the process. As with our birth, our death is in God's hands. We finally must surrender to his will even if we have spent a lifetime refusing to do so.

We do, however, control our destination. How we leave isn't up to us; where we spend eternity is -- and that depends on our relationship with Jesus.

If I drop dead tomorrow, at least I know I died in good health.
-- Pro football coach Bum Phillips after a physical

When you go isn't up to you; where you go is.

CLOTHES HORSE

Read Genesis 37:1-11.

"Israel loved Joseph more than all his children, because he was the son of his old age: and he made him a coat of many colours" (v. 3 KJV).

Al Ciraldo was a man of many sterling qualities, but he was certainly not a clothes horse.

Ciraldo was the radio voice of the Yellow Jackets for 38 seasons, a figure and voice so well-known and so beloved that he is a member of Tech's Hall of Fame. From 1974 to 2003, his color commentator was former Jacket quarterback Kim King. Shortly after King started, the manager of the flagship station, WGST, told King he was "tired of going to the games and seeing you guys wear different clothes." King understood what the manager was saying: that "Al was still wearing those 1940 suits he had." As King put it, "Al was not too extravagant with money, particularly when it came to personal comfort things."

So the manager set up a deal with Muse's to get the announcing duo some slacks and a matching blazer. A salesman was waiting for them when they arrived, and King selected "a nice pair of light gray wool slacks and a really nice blue blazer." The coat cost about $400 and the slacks about $90, pretty good money then. When it was Al's turn, he turned to the salesman and said, "I think I'll just take the cash." He pocketed the money and didn't buy the clothes.

The station manager was not exactly overjoyed at how the deal went down, especially when he showed up at the next game to see King all spiffy in his blazer and slacks and Al still wearing his wide-lapel, doubled-breasted, 1940s suit.

Contemporary society proclaims that it's all about the clothes. Buy that new suit or dress, those new shoes, and all the sparkling accessories, and you'll be a new person. The changes are only cosmetic, though; under those clothes, you're the same person. Consider Joseph, for instance, prancing about in his pretty new clothes; he was still a spoiled tattletale.

Jesus never taught that we should run around half-naked or wear only second-hand clothes from the local mission. He did warn us, though, against making consumer items such as clothes a priority in our lives. A follower of Christ seeks to emulate Jesus not through material, superficial means such as wearing special clothing like a robe and sandals. Rather, the disciple desires to match Jesus' inner beauty and serenity -- whether the clothes the Christian wears are the sables of a king or the rags of a pauper.

You can't call [golf] a sport. You don't run, jump, you don't shoot, you don't pass. All you have to do is buy some clothes that don't match.
-- Former major leaguer Steve Sax

Where Jesus is concerned, clothes don't make the person; faith does.

DAY 10

SMILING FACES

Read Philippians 4:4-7.

"Rejoice in the Lord always. I will say it again: Rejoice!"
(v. 4)

Wes Hodges had a loopy smile, but he considered it a blessing that he had one at all.

As a freshman in 2004, Hodges started for Tech at third base and hit a grand slam in his first game. His season came to a sudden and dangerous end on May 11, though, when he was hit in the face by a pitch in the Georgia game. Rushed to a hospital emergency room, he was so eager to leave he yanked the IV out of his arm and walked out around 4 a.m.

Later that morning his parents took him to an eye doctor, who delivered the good news that while the baseball had broken Hodges' sinus wall in three places and the orbital bone below his left eye, his eyesight wasn't permanently damaged. The doctor did say that had the pitch hit him a centimeter higher, Hodges' baseball career would have been over.

The doctor recommended surgery to remove some bone fragments, but after extensive prayer, the family decided against an operation. The injury healed without it, and Hodges returned for the 2005 season. He led the Jackets with a .397 average and was All-ACC and second-team All-America. After his junior season, he received a million-dollar bonus to sign with the Cleveland Indians.

The only lingering evidence of Hodges' awful injury is his smile; the left side doesn't extend as high or as wide as the right side. But that doesn't keep Hodges from smiling. "I'm counting my blessings," he said during the 2005 season.

What does your smile say about you? What is it that makes you smile in the first place? Your dad's corny jokes? Don Knotts as Barney Fife? Your children or grandchildren? Your pal's bad imitations? Do you hoard your smile or do you -- like Wes Hodges --give it away easily even when you've had some tough times?

When you smile, the ones who love you and whom you love can't help but return the favor -- and the joy. It's like turning on a bright light in a world threatened by darkness.

Besides, you have good reason to walk around all the time with a smile on your face not because of something you have done but rather because of one basic, unswerving truth: God loves you. As a result of his great love for you, God acted through Jesus to give you free and eternal salvation. That should certainly make you smile.

The bat is gone but the smile remains.
-- Baseball Hall of Famer Willie Stargell

It so overused it's become a cliché, but it's true nevertheless: Smile! God loves you.

DAY 11

BE KIND

Read Ephesians 4:17-32.

"Be kind and compassionate to one another, forgiving each other, just as in Christ God forgave you" (v. 32).

While opposing cornerbacks would disagree, the greatest receiver in Georgia Tech football history was at heart a kind person – so kind that he spent a summer while he was at Tech building toilets for those who didn't have them.

When Calvin Johnson declared for the draft after his junior season in 2006, he was first in Tech history in career receiving yards, second in receptions, and first in touchdown receptions. He won the Biletnikoff Award in 2006 as the best wide receiver in the country; he was also named the ACC Player of the Year. He was All-America in 2005 and 2006 and All-ACC three times.

Austin Murphy wrote that Johnson left "in his wake a series of traumatized cornerbacks whose thought balloons . . . would all say the same thing: But . . . but . . . I had great coverage!"

Johnson never intentionally set out to humiliate anyone, though. "He always had a kind nature about him," his mother said. She said he picked opponents up off the ground not to show off but simply because "sportsmanship was important to him." Johnson played football at Tech following the lesson his parents instilled in him: "I always told him," his mother said, "if you treat people the way you want to be treated, things will work out."

Johnson illustrated his "kindness-toward-others" philosophy

during the summer of 2006 when he was given a choice of two projects: help with the construction of some environmentally friendly luxury condos or build solar latrines for Bolivians. He chose the latter to help someone less fortunate than he.

We may all talk about kindness, but moving beyond the talk to demonstrating kindness to others is so exceptional in our world that we take notice of it; witness the inclusion in his online biography of Calvin Johnson's building latrines not from any desire for personal gain but out of a realization of a need. The person who finds a wallet with cash in it and returns it to the owner merits a spot on the evening news. So does the millionaire who gives a big chunk of change to a hospital or a charity.

Practicing kindness is difficult because it requires that we move beyond our own selves to the recognition of the needs of others; a kind person places others first. In an impersonal world, a kind person goes to the time and the trouble to establish personal contact – just as Jesus did and just as God did when he sent Jesus to us.

You can motivate players better with kind words than with a whip.
– Former coach Bud Wilkinson

Practicing kindness is hard because it requires us to place others first, exactly the way Jesus lived among us.

MAKING PLANS

Read Psalm 33:1-15.

"The plans of the Lord stand firm forever, the purposes of his heart through all generations" (v. 11).

The media had already dubbed the Georgia Bulldogs of 1927 the best football team in the nation. Thus, Tech was a decided underdog on Dec. 3 for the last game of the season. But Coach William Alexander had a plan.

A month before the Georgia game, Alexander told his squad, "I will give you a plan that will win the last four games on our schedule." Al Thomy wrote, "The players were curious. The plan, the plan, what was the plan? They could not wait."

Alexander unveiled his plan to his players after the Vanderbilt game. He pulled a sheet of paper from his pocket and read off twelve names. "These men will report to me on the field," he said. "These 12 men will be the team that plays Georgia on Dec. 3." He then scanned the paper again and called out eighteen names. "These men," he said, "will make up the team that plays LSU, Oglethorpe, and Auburn. They will report to Coach Bill Fincher. They will be expected to win their three games." The rest of the squad would run the Georgia offense and defense for four weeks.

"The plan cannot fail," Alexander concluded.

It didn't. Fincher's players drubbed LSU 23-0, Oglethorpe 19-7, and Auburn 18-0. With four weeks to practice for Georgia, Alexander's players won 12-0, eliminating the Bulldogs from the Rose Bowl and national title consideration.

Jack "Stumpy" Thomason, who returned an interception 58 yards for Tech's second touchdown, said that with his plan Alexander "didn't miss a trick."

Successful living takes planning. You go to school to improve your chances for a better paying job. You use blueprints to build your home. You plan for retirement. You map out your vacation to have the best time. You even plan your children -- sometimes.

Your best-laid plans, however, sometimes get wrecked by events and circumstances beyond your control. The economy goes into the tank; a debilitating illness strikes; a hurricane hits. Life is capricious and thus no plans – not even your best ones -- are foolproof.

But you don't have to go it alone. God has plans for your life that guarantee success as God defines it if you will make him your planning partner. God's plan for your life includes joy, love, peace, kindness, gentleness, and faithfulness, all the elements necessary for truly successful living for today and for all eternity. And God's plan will not fail.

If you don't know where you are going, you will wind up somewhere else.

-- *Yogi Berra*

Your plans may ensure a successful life;
God's plans will ensure a successful eternity.

IT'S THE TRUTH

Read Matthew 5:33-37.

*"Simply let your 'Yes' be 'Yes,' and your 'No,' 'No';
anything beyond this comes from the evil one" (v. 37).*

What do you do with a player who tells the coach right in front of the whole team that she's not telling the truth? In the case of Janie Mitchell, you applaud her.

Mitchell finished her Tech basketball career in 2007-08 with 1,422 points, seventh-best in school history, and 704 rebounds, ninth best in Yellow Jacket history. As a senior, she averaged 16.4 points and six rebounds per game, both of which led the team.

The Yellow Jackets of 2006-07 were in trouble after Vanderbilt scored 26 straight points against them in the last half to whip them easily 72-55 on Jan. 21. After starting the season 8-3, the Jackets had fallen to a 10-8 record.

In the locker room after the game, Mitchell looked around and saw a broken team that was getting used to losing. Coach MaChelle Joseph saw the same thing, so she tried to encourage her discouraged players. "Keep your heads up," she said. "We are a good team. We just have to believe in ourselves."

But Mitchell saw a team that was consistently beating itself. "We're not a good team," she piped up. "We have got to quit saying we are a good team. We've got to put it out there on the floor."

Her teammates listened. "We all rallied around her and agreed," senior Stephanie Higgs said. The Jackets went on to win

20 games and made it into the NCAA tournament for the third time in school history.

And the turning point was the night a player insisted her coach wasn't telling the truth.

No, that dress doesn't make you look fat. But, officer, I wasn't speeding. I didn't get the project finished because I've been at the hospital every night with my ailing grandmother. What good-looking guy? I didn't notice.

Sometimes we lie to spare the feelings of others; more often, though, we lie to bail ourselves out of a jam, to make ourselves look better to others, or to gain the upper hand over someone.

But Jesus admonishes us to tell the truth. Frequently in our faith life we fret about what is right and what is wrong, but we can have no such ambivalence when it comes to telling the truth or lying. God and his son are so closely associated with the truth that lying is ultimately attributed to the devil ("the evil one"). Given his character, God cannot lie; given his character, the devil lies as a way of life. Given your character, which is it?

Trampling on the truth has become as common place as overpaid athletes and bad television.

-- *Hockey coach Dan Bauer*

**Jesus declared himself to be the truth,
so whose side are we on when we lie?**

DAY 14

THE GREATEST

Read Mark 9:33-37.

"'If anyone wants to be first, he must be the very last, and the servant of all'" (v. 35).

Considering the sheer drama and the implications, Tech's 1990 win over top-ranked Virginia may well be the greatest football game in the school's history. On that Nov. 3 afternoon, the ACC championship was at stake and – as it turned out – so was the national championship.

Virginia led early 13-0, but the resilient Jackets drove 75 yards with quarterback Shawn Jones scrambling for the last 23. Virginia responded to lead 21-7 before Jones hit Jerry Gilchrist for his first career touchdown, a 43-yarder. Virginia then scored right before the half to lead at the break 28-14.

On the first play of the second half, linebacker Calvin Tiggle recovered a fumble. Gilchrist scored on a 12-yard flanker reverse, and then Jones, who admitted he was having "a lot of fun," hit Emmett Merchant for a 26-yard score. The game was tied at 28 late in the third quarter.

The thrilling roller-coaster ride continued when Virginia took a 35-28 lead in the fourth quarter. Tech answered yet again with a 74-yard drive, fullback William Bell scoring from the eight. Scott Sisson's 32-yard field goal gave Tech its first lead, but with 2:34 left to play, a Virginia field goal tied the game at 38.

Jones and the Jackets stormed down the field. Only seven

seconds were left when Sisson's 37-yard kick split the uprights, the moment so dramatic that many Jackets on the sideline couldn't watch. Tech had a 41-38 win that propelled the Jackets into the national championship discussion in what could well be considered the greatest Tech football game of them all.

We all want to be the greatest. The goal for the Yellow Jackets and their fans every season is at least the conference championship. The competition at work is to be the most productive sales person on the staff or the Teacher of the Year. In other words, we define being the greatest in terms of the struggle for personal success. It's nothing new; the disciples saw greatness in the same way.

As Jesus illustrated, though, greatness in the Kingdom of God has nothing to do with the world's understanding of success. Rather, the greatest are those who channel their ambition toward the furtherance of Christ's kingdom through love and service, rather than their own advancement, which is a complete reversal of status and values as the world sees them.

After all, who could be greater than the person who has Jesus for a brother and God for a father? And that's every one of us.

My goal was to be the greatest athlete that ever lived.
-- *Babe Didrikson Zaharias*

**To be great for God has nothing to do
with personal advancement and everything to do
with the advancement of Christ's kingdom.**

DAY 15

CHEERS

Read Matthew 21:1-11.

"The crowds that went ahead of him and those that followed shouted" (v. 9).

The oldest documented football cheer in Georgia Tech history is not likely to make a comeback anytime soon.

Frank Markert was the center on the Georgia Tech teams of 1901-02 when the first cheer surfaced. That cheer was not the only "first" he saw. The 1902 team devised a revolutionary play: an off-tackle run. "That might not sound like much today," Market recalled once, but the play changed the game because "it took some of the emphasis from the mass play or the wedge."

Markert was also present when the first forward pass was thrown against Tech, also in 1902. "It certainly startled us when St. Albans, a small school from Virginia, pulled it on us," Markert said. The pass – against the rules – was a short pass to the half-back, and Tech's player-coach objected. "He'd never seen it before." The officials, though, let the play stand. "They said it was a lateral pass which was legal instead of a forward pass."

Markert was part of yet another pivotal first in Tech football history. After his senior year in 1903, other players and he met with some alumni in the home of school president Lyman Hall and decided to offer the head coaching job to John Heisman of Clemson. The vote moved Tech into the big-time since Heisman was the school's first full-time, paid football coach.

But that first cheer in 1902? Markert said it went, "Boom-a-lacka, Boom-a-lacka, Bow Wow Wow. Chick-a-lacka, Tick-a-lacka, Tow Tow Tow. Boom-a-lacka, Chick-a-Lacka, Who are We? Georgia School of Technology."

Chances are you go to work every day, do your job well, and then go home to your family. This country couldn't run without you; you're indispensable to the nation's efficiency. Even so, nobody cheers for you – shouting Boom-a-lacka, Boom-a-lacka -- or waves pompoms in your face. Your name probably will never elicit a standing ovation if a PA announcer ever calls it.

It's just as well, since public opinion is notoriously fickle. Consider what happened to Jesus. When he entered Jerusalem, he was the object of raucous cheering and an impromptu parade. The crowd's adulation reached such a frenzy they tore branches off trees and threw their clothes on the ground.

Five days later the crowd shouted again, only this time they screamed for Jesus' execution.

So don't worry too much about not having your personal set of cheering fans. Remember that you do have one personal cheerleader who will never stop pulling for you: God.

A cheerleader is a dreamer that never gives up.

– Source unknown

Just like the sports stars, you do have a personal cheerleader: God.

DAY 16

HOMELESS

Read Matthew 8:18-22.

"Jesus replied, 'Foxes have holes and birds of the air have nests, but the Son of Man has no place to lay his head'" (v. 20).

Basketball began at Georgia Tech in 1906, but the early teams were homeless, lacking a permanent on-campus facility in which to play.

On Feb. 17, 1906, Tech's first basketball team lost to Auburn in Peachtree Auditorium. Despite a 2-1 record that first season, the sport generated little interest among the students because the games weren't played on campus. Not until 1909 would Tech play another intercollegiate basketball game, meeting Mercer in Cable Piano Company's hall on Broad Street.

Tech dropped the program again until 1913. The old school foundry on Cherry Street had received a face-lift and had been renamed the Crystal Palace. On Feb. 13, 1913, Tech hosted Clemson at the Palace for the school's first-ever on-campus game.

The program lapsed again until 1919-20 when legendary coach William Alexander organized a team. Through 1923, the basketball team played its "home" games at various places around the city. In October 1923, athletic director J.B. Crenshaw entreated the athletic board and the trustees to construct a field house "to relieve our present very deplorable situation." What Crenshaw got was a temporary wooden gym that seated about 2,500.

The facility proved to be temporary indeed when it burned down in 1931, sending the Jackets to City Auditorium until the Civil Works Administration constructed a Naval Armory on the site of the former gymnasium in time for the 1934-35 season.

Finally, in 1939, Heisman Gymnasium, a bandbox that seated fewer than 1,800, was constructed. More than thirty years after the program began, Tech's basketball team finally had a permanent on-campus home of its own.

Rock bottom in America has a face: the bag lady pushing a shopping cart; the scruffy guy with a beard and a backpack at the interstate exit holding a cardboard sign. Look closer at that bag lady or that scruffy guy, though, and you may see desperate women with children fleeing violence, veterans haunted by their combat experiences, or sick or injured workers.

Few of us are indifferent to the homeless when we're around them. They often raise quite strong passions, whether we regard them as a ministry or a nuisance. They trouble us, perhaps because we realize that we're only one catastrophic illness and a few paychecks away from joining them. They remind us, therefore, of how tenuous our hold upon material success really is.

But they also stir our compassion because we serve a Lord who – like them -- had no home, and for whom, the homeless, too, are his children.

Some people beat up on the homeless for sport.
-- Maryland State Sen. Lisa Gladden

Because they, too, are God's children, the homeless merit our compassion, not our scorn.

DAY 17

MAMA'S BOY

Read John 19:25-30.

"Near the cross of Jesus stood his mother" (v. 25).

Perhaps no coiffure in Tech athletic history caused more of a stir than did Coach Pepper Rodgers' perm. It took his mama to kill it.

Rodgers was a backup quarterback and placekicker on Georgia Tech's 1952 national champions. He became a Tech legend when his late field goal defeated Baylor 17-14 in the 1952 Orange Bowl to cap a furious Tech comeback. Rodgers' kick marked the first time a field goal had decided an Orange Bowl.

Rodgers came home to the Institute in 1974 after stints as head coach at Kansas and UCLA. He is certainly the most colorful coach in Tech history, fully embracing the lifestyle of the day. As Adam Van Brimmer put it, Rodgers "rode a motorcycle to the office, shunned socks, and permed his hair."

Tech fans generally could handle the motorcycle and the rest, but that perm just didn't sit well with the faithful. Rodgers, however, refused to change his do until after his signature win, the 23-14 upset of 11th-ranked Notre Dame in 1976. As Rodgers' mother, Louise, filed out of Grant Field after the game, she heard a woman say, "That was a good win, but I still don't like Pepper's hair." Mrs. Louise retorted, "Maybe he doesn't like your hair." "Who are you?" the woman shot back. Then came the answer that doomed the perm: "I'm his aunt."

That his own mother wouldn't claim him because of his hair dismayed the coach. "That was the demise of my permanent," he said. "I cut my hair the next day."

Mamas such as Mrs. Louise often face conflicts and problems in dealing with and standing by their children. No mother in history, though, has faced a challenge to match that of Mary, whom God chose to be the mother of Jesus. Like mamas and their children throughout time, Mary experienced both joy and perplexity in her relationship with her son.

To the end, though, Mary stood by her boy. She followed him all the way to his execution, an act of love and bravery since Jesus was condemned as an enemy of the Roman Empire.

But just as mothers like Mary – and perhaps yours -- would apparently do anything for their children, so will God do anything out of love for his children. After all, that was God on the cross at the foot of which Mary stood, and he was dying for you, one of his children.

Everyone should find time to write and to go see their mother. I think that's healthy.

– Bear Bryant

**Mamas often sacrifice for their children,
but God, too, will do anything out of love
for his children, including dying on a cross.**

DAY 18

RUNNING FOR YOUR LIFE

Read John 20:1-10.

"Peter and the other disciple started for the tomb. Both were running, but the other disciple outran Peter and reached the tomb first" (vv. 3-4).

After what they did to the Bulldogs, it's a wonder the Tech football team didn't leave the team buses in Athens and run back to campus.

On Saturday, Nov. 29, 2008, Paul Johnson's Yellow Jackets ran over, under, around, and through the hapless Georgia defense and defeated the Dogs 45-42. The offense that couldn't possibly work at the major college level rolled up 409 yards on the ground, including an unbelievable 201-1 edge in the third quarter.

Redshirt freshman Roddy Jones romped for 214 yards while Jonathan Dwyer galloped for 144 yards and two touchdowns on 20 carries. Jones set a school record by averaging 16.4 yards per carry on only 13 rushes.

With his team trailing 28-12 at halftime, Johnson told the Jackets, "Hey, it's sixty minutes. Anybody who came over here and didn't think it's going to be that kind of game, don't come back out." The first coach in Tech history to win nine games his first season reminded his team they got the ball to start the second half and would go down the field and score. "I didn't know it'd be on one play," Johnson said.

But it was. On Tech's first snap, Dwyer went 60 yards for a

touchdown. Tech scored three touchdown in less than seven minutes and added a field goal for a 38-28 lead.

Even after Georgia closed to 38-35, the Jacket running game couldn't be stopped. Jones went 54 yards for the game-winning touchdown only six plays after Georgia had scored.

The Jackets simply ran wild.

Hit the ground running -- every morning that's what you do as you leave the house and re-enter the rat race. You run errands, you run though a presentation; you give someone a run for his money; you always want to be in the running and never run-of-the-mill.

You're always running toward something, such as your goals, or away from something, such as your past. Many of us spend much of our lives foolhardily attempting to run away from God, the purposes he has for us, and the blessings he is waiting to pour out. No matter how hard or how far you run, though, you can never outrun yourself or God. God keeps pace with you, calling you in the short run to take care of the long run by falling to your knees and running for your life -- to Jesus. By falling to your knees you run all the way to glory.

It is impossible to win the race unless you venture to run, impossible to win the victory unless you dare to battle.
-- Amway founder Richard DeVos

You can run all the way to eternity
by going to your knees.

DAY 19

NEVER TOO LATE

Read Genesis 21:1-7.

"And [Sarah] added, 'Who would have said to Abraham that Sarah would nurse children? Yet I have borne him a son in his old age'" (v. 7).

Graduation Day on The Flats and there were Joe Hamilton and Brian Oliver, two of the most famous athletes in Georgia Tech history, making their family, coaches, themselves, Tech administrators, and NCAA statisticians everywhere happy by receiving their diplomas. Only, Hamilton was 30 and Oliver was 39.

"It took years of overtime," but in August 2007, two of Tech's finest finally could call themselves college graduates. As a senior quarterback in 1999, Hamilton was the runner-up for the Heisman Trophy after setting ACC career records for total offense, touchdown passes, and total touchdowns. Oliver was a basketball All-America in 1989 and 1990 and the team captain of the 1990 ACC Champions that advanced to the Final Four.

Despite their athletic accomplishments, though, both men felt keenly the absence of a college diploma. Oliver eventually played basketball in Europe, living most of the year in Italy, which hindered his passing college courses in Atlanta. With his wife encouraging him, he used his vacation time to attend summer school. Hamilton gave motivational speeches to children, but he always harbored a secret worry that a child would ask him if he had earned his college degree.

Tech sports publicist Mike Stamus said Oliver's 17-year gap between his final college game and his final college exam was unique. "We've had a few others (such as Eddie Lee Ivery who graduated in 1992, 14 years after his senior season), but nobody like this," Stamus said.

For Joe Hamilton and Brian Oliver, it was never too late to finish what they had started.

Getting that college degree. Running a marathon. Getting married. Starting a new career. Though we may make all kinds of excuses, it's often never too late for life-changing decisions and milestones.

This is especially true in our faith life, which is based on God's promises. Abraham was 100 and Sarah was 90 when their first child was born. They were old folks even by the Bible's standards at the dawn of history. But God had promised them a child and just as God always does, he kept his promise no matter how unlikely it seemed.

God has made us all a promise of new life and hope through Jesus Christ. At any time in our lives – today even -- we can regret the things we have done wrong and the way we have lived, ask God in Jesus' name to forgive us for them, and discover a new way of living – forever.

It's never too late to change. God promised.

It's never too late to achieve success in sports.
    -- Brooke de Lench, writer and lecturer on children and sports

**It's never too late to change a life
by turning it over to Jesus.**

DAY 20

DREAM WORLD

Read Joel 2:26-28.

"Your old men will dream dreams, your young men will see visions" (v. 28).

Bryan Shelton sold Alison Silverio on a dream. Four years later, that dream came true with the first NCAA team national championship in Tech sports history.

An All-American tennis player at Tech in 1988 who took over the women's program in 1999, Shelton recruited Silverio out of Louisville, Ohio, by repeatedly telling her she could be the foundation that helped build Tech into a national champion. It certainly was a dream since the women's tennis program had been moribund until Shelton took over.

But on May 22, 2007, senior Silverio defeated her UCLA counterpart 6-1 in the third set to clinch a 4-2 Tech win and the national championship Shelton had promised.

Silverio joined her teammates – Tarryn Rudman, Kirsten Flower, Kristi Miller, Whitney McCray, and Amanda Craddock – in hoisting the national championship trophy in Athens. "It has been an unbelievable four years," she said. "I came to the program as a freshman and we were ranked 42 in the nation and to end up my senior year in the number one position. It is an amazing accomplishment."

Tech was in trouble early against UCLA with a surprise loss in doubles. With a second loss in singles, the pressure fell squarely on Miller and Silverio. "I have never seen Ally lose a deciding match, and that was what it was," Miller said. "She has done it so many times, and I had complete faith in her. . . . She always comes through."

She did – and so did the entire Tech team to make the dream come true.

You have dreams. Maybe to make a lot of money. Write the great American novel. Or have the fairy-tale romance. But dreams often are crushed beneath the weight of everyday living; reality, not dreams, comes to occupy your time, attention, and effort. You've come to understand that achieving your dreams requires a combination of persistence, timing, and providence.

But what if your dreams don't come true because they're not good enough? That is, they're based on the alluring but unreliable promises of the world rather than the true promises of God, which are a sure thing.

God calls us to great achievements because God's dreams for us are greater than our dreams for ourselves. Such greatness occurs, though, only when our dreams and God's will for our lives are the same. Your dreams should be worthy of your best – and worthy of God's involvement in making them come true.

An athlete cannot run with money in his pocket. He must run with hope in his heart and dreams in his head.
-- Olympic Gold Medalist Emil Zatopek

**Dreams based on the world's promises
are often crushed; those based on God's promises
are a sure thing.**

DAY 21

BACK FROM THE DEAD

Read Matthew 28:1-10.

"He is not here; he has risen, just as he said. Come and see the place where he lay" (v. 6).

We were so dead in the water." So said head coach Bobby Cremins about his 1995-96 Tech basketball team. But the squad resurrected itself and added a glorious chapter to roundball lore on The Flats.

Cremins spoke about December as the 6-7 Jackets prepared for the daunting ACC schedule that lay ahead. "We knew going into ACC play that if we didn't correct some things we were going to get hammered, and I mean hammered," Cremins said.

Cremins had had two strong recruiting classes and expected good things for 1995-96. But there they were dead in the water until "just as things appeared dark and distraught, the Jackets rose from the grave." They went 13-3 in league play and won Georgia Tech's first outright ACC regular-season title.

Point guard Stephon Marbury said the turnaround was the result of "guts and heart." Plus a severe tongue lashing from Cremins, who "really chewed us out and showed us what to work on."

After the Jackets whipped Clemson to win the league title, Cremins surveyed the season. "If you had told me in December that I'd be standing here as the coach of the ACC regular-season champions, I would have told you you're crazy," he said.

The Jackets defeated Austin Peay 90-79 in the first round of the NCAA Tournament and then set a Southeast region record with sixteen three-pointers in a 103-89 thrashing of Boston College. The magnificent last-half run ended in the Sweet Sixteen.

"I'll never forget this team," Cremins said, this team that came back from the dead.

All of this language of resurrection is figurative, of course; no one on that great Tech team was literally dead. What was apparently dead in December was Tech's basketball season. We often speak figuratively of resurrected careers in sports. We use resurrection language when a team comes from way behind to win a game or salvage a season.

While literal resurrections occur in the New Testament, one in particular stands alone. All others are merely the postponement of death, but when Jesus walked out of that tomb on the first Easter morning, he threw off not only his burial cloths but death itself. On that day, God created something new: the resurrection life that one day will be the only one.

That's because resurrection is a fact of life for the followers of Jesus. When Christ left that tomb behind, he also left death behind for all who believe that he is indeed the savior of the world.

After crucifixion comes resurrection.

-- Greek sprinter Costas Kenteris

Jesus' resurrection forever ended death's hold on life; life has won.

LIMITED-TIME OFFER

Read Psalm 103.

"As for man, his days are like grass, he flourishes like a flower of the field; the wind blows over it and it is gone. . . . But from everlasting to everlasting the Lord's love is with those who fear him" (vv. 15-17).

Clint Castleberry could have been the greatest back the South has produced," wrote Al Thomy. Castleberry's No. 19 is the only retired jersey number in Georgia Tech's football history even though he played only one season. So what happened?

As a freshman running back in 1942, Castleberry led Tech to a 9-1 season, a berth in the Cotton Bowl, and a No. 5 national ranking. He finished third in the voting for the Heisman Trophy. One writer said he "blazed across the football field like a 'crazed jackrabbit.'" He had played only one game – a 15-0 win over Auburn – when Notre Dame scout Wayne Millner warned his head coach that "the most dangerous runner in America" was on his way to South Bend. The coach's anxiety was merited; Tech won 13-6 as Castleberry passed for one touchdown and ran for another.

Castleberry rushed for 466 yards that remarkable season, averaging 8.5 yards per carry. He was a sure tackler at safety and the team's punt returner. "That was a thing of beauty, watching him return a punt," said his coach at Tech, Dwight Keith. "He never let the ball hit the ground, taking all kicks on the run."

So why was No. 19's career on The Flats so short? After the 1942 season, he enlisted in the air corps. While he was flying over the Mediterranean, his plane disappeared without a trace. "He was a star on the horizon; he was here, he made things happen and then he was gone," remembered teammate Jim Luck.

A heart attack, cancer, or an accident will probably take -- or has already taken -- someone you know or love who is "too young to die" such as Clint Castleberry.

The death of a younger person never seems to "make sense." That's because such a death belies the common view of death as the natural end of a life lived well and lived long. Moreover, you can't see the whole picture as God does, so you can't know how the death furthers God's kingdom.

At such a time, you can seize the comforting truth that God is in control and therefore everything will be all right one day. You can also gain a sense of urgency in your own life by appreciating that God's offer of life through Jesus Christ is a limited-time offer that expires at your death – and there's no guarantee about when that will be.

No one knows when he or she is going to die, so if we're going to accept Christ, we'd better not wait because death can come in the blink of an eye.

-- Bobby Bowden

**God offers you life through Jesus Christ, but you
must accept it before your death when it expires.**

STRANGE BUT TRUE

Read 1 Corinthians 1:18-31.

"The message of the cross is foolishness to those who are perishing, but to us who are being saved it is the power of God" (v. 18).

Is the strangest play in college football history the finish to the 1982 Stanford-Cal game when the Stanford band rushed onto the field and California scored? Maybe not. Consider the 1904 Georgia Tech-Georgia game.

The two teams played at the baseball field in Piedmont Park, and late in the first half Georgia lined up to punt from its own end zone. The punter stood between the goal posts, which were on the goal line then, and a high fence. To his dismay, his punt struck the goal posts and bounced over the fence.

The players stood around, open-mouthed, wondering what to do next until the referee decided that since there were no end zones, the ball was still in play. Legendary sportswriter Grantland Rice recorded the strange scene that followed: "Suddenly both elevens made a dash at the slippery fence, sixteen feet high. . . . No sooner would a begrimed athlete scramble to the top than he would be yanked back by some rival."

Finally, Tech's Red Wilson used a stump to propel himself over the fence with a Georgia player and the referee right behind. The ball was nowhere in sight, and only after a search of several minutes did Wilson find the ball buried in some deep grass. He fell on it and the ref signaled touchdown.

Nobody else had seen Wilson's feat, and, according to Rice, only when he "finally reappeared over the wall with the missing sphere under his arm [did] a storm of cheers roll across the battlefield."

Life is just strange, isn't it? How else to explain the college bowl situation, tattoos, curling, tofu, and teenagers? Isn't it strange that today we have more ways to stay in touch with each other yet are losing the intimacy of personal contact? Who could ever explain Dr. Phil, Christopher Walken, the presidential primaries, and Scientology?

And how strange is it that God let himself be killed by being nailed to a couple of pieces of wood? Think about that: the creator and ruler of the entire universe suffering the indignity and the torture of being labeled a common criminal and then executed in the manner reserved for the most ignominious of offenders.

But there's more. The cross, a symbol of disgrace, defeat, and death, ultimately became a worldwide symbol of hope, victory, and life. That's really strange.

So is the fact that love drove God to that cross. It's strange – but it's true.

It may sound strange, but many champions are made champions by setbacks.

-- *Olympic champion Bob Richards*

It's strange but true: God allowed himself to be killed on a cross because of his great love for you.

DAY 24

HEART OF THE MATTER

Read 1 Samuel 13:1-14.

"The Lord has sought out a man after his own heart" (v. 14).

It took more than hitting, fielding, and pitching for the Jackets to win the 2005 ACC baseball tournament. It took a lot of heart.

The Yellow Jackets were the regular-season champions, but they didn't exactly get off to a rip-roaring start in the tournament, falling behind 7-0 to Wake Forest in the opening game. Instead of sitting back, though, and riding their regular-season accomplishments into the NCAA tournament, the Jackets put together one of their greatest rallies ever to clip Wake 9-8.

But Tech wasn't through falling behind; in fact, they had just started. The Jackets met FSU in the second round and trailed 4-0 headed into the bottom of the seventh. That's when Coach Danny Hall's bunch showed its heart again. The Jackets scored five times, sending ten batters to the plate. They slapped out seven singles with Whit Robbins driving in Steve Blackwood with what proved to be the winning run in the 5-4 victory.

Then in the finals, the Jackets had to come from behind again – twice. They trailed Virginia 1-0 and 3-2 before rallying in the bottom of the seventh. Robbins scored when Jeff Kindel drew a bases-loaded walk. Second baseman Mike Trapani later scored on a wild pitch, and relief pitchers Jordan Crews and Matt Wieters made the lead stand up.

"That's the kind of stuff that we've been doing all year," Trapani said. "I've never been on a team like this." Tournament MVP Tyler Greene agreed the team was special in that the guys "keep battling."

They had heart and it showed.

We all face defeat even as the Yellow Jackets did in that 2005 ACC Tournament. Sometimes, even though we fight with all we have, we lose. Even Tech loses games.

At some time, you probably have admitted you were whipped no matter how much it hurt. Always in your life, though, you have known that you would fight for some things with all your heart and never give them up: your family, your country, your friends, your core beliefs.

God should be on that list too. God seeks men and women who will never turn their back on him because they are people after God's own heart. That is, they will never betray God with their unbelief; they will never lose their childlike trust in God; they will never cease to love God with all their heart.

They are lifetime members of God's team; it's a mighty good one to be on, but it takes heart.

It is not the size of a man but the size of his heart that matters.
-- *Evander Holyfield*

To be on God's team requires the heart of a champion.

DAY 25

CAN'T GO WRONG

Read Galatians 6:7-10.

"Let us not grow weary in doing what is right, for we will reap at harvest time, if we do not give up" (v. 9 NRSV).

Georgia Tech President Blake Van Leer was determined to do the right thing even if it killed him – and it probably did.

Van Leer took the reins of the Institute in 1944; as Tech's president he experienced in 1955 what he called "the toughest four days of my life."

As was typical during the 1950s, Tech had a great football season. The Jackets tied Tennessee and lost only to Auburn 14-12. After a 21-3 pasting of Georgia, the Jackets accepted a bid to play Pittsburgh in the Sugar Bowl. That's when trouble arose.

Van Leer, Coach Bobby Dodd, and other Tech officials knew that the Panthers had an African-American player, but thought nothing of it since Georgia had been playing racially mixed teams for several seasons. But politics got tossed into the mix, and Gov. Marvin Griffin expressed his opposition to Tech's playing the game. The Institute's student body responded by marching on the Capitol and hanging the governor in effigy.

Van Leer stood his ground by issuing a statement that ended the matter as far as he and Georgia Tech were concerned: "I am 60 years old and have never broken a contract. I do not intend to start now."

The Board of Regents met, after which the chairman declared

Tech could play the game. The Jackets won it 7-0 on a Wade Mitchell touchdown.

Doing the right thing cost Van Leer. Six weeks after his showdown with the state government and the regents, he died of a cerebral hemorrhage.

Doing the right thing is easy when it's little stuff. Giving the quarter back when the cashier gives you too much change, helping a lost child at the mall, or putting a few bucks in the honor box at your favorite fishing hole.

But what about when it costs you? Every day you have multiple chances to do the right thing; in every instance, you have a choice: right or wrong. The factors that weigh into your decisions – including the personal cost to you – reveal much about your character.

Does your doing the right thing ever depend upon your calculation of the odds of getting caught? In the world's eyes, you can't go wrong doing wrong when you won't get caught. That passes for the world's slippery, situational ethics, but it doesn't pass muster with God.

In God's eyes, you can't go wrong doing right. Ever.

I won't tolerate a womanizer, I won't tolerate a drunk, and I won't tolerate a cheater. Those are the things that'll cost you your job.
--Bobby Bowden to his assistant coaches

As far as God is concerned, you can never go wrong doing right.

A JOYFUL NOISE

Read Psalm 100.

"Make a joyful noise to the Lord, all the earth" (v. 1 NRSV).

If it's game day at Grant Field, it must be noisy, and the noisiest bunch of all dresses alike and sits together. It's the Georgia Tech Yellow Jacket Marching Band.

The Tech band was founded in 1908 by fourteen students led by Robert "Biddy" Bidez, who served as the band leader until he graduated in 1912. Mike Greenblatt followed him as Tech's first professional bandleader. He made the first arrangement and score of "Ramblin' Wreck." Frank Roman became the band director in 1914, and he adapted and copyrighted "Ramblin' Wreck," providing the version that is popular today.

Tech became the first college in the South to have its music recorded when in 1925 the Columbia Gramophone Company issued a recording of Tech songs made by the band and the Men's Glee Club.

A new day arrived for the band in 1954 when trombonist Teresa Thomas and flutist Paula Stevenson, two of the nine distaff students enrolled at Tech, became the first female members of the band.

The Tech band pulled off one of the most famous pranks in school history in 1992 during halftime of the Georgia game in Athens. As the band took the field, several band members covered up the Georgia logo at midfield with a tarp bearing the Georgia Tech logo. The band's performance was drowned out by a chorus of hearty boos from the home crowd, which completely delighted the band members.

That was one of the few occasions when the noise elicited by the Tech marching band wasn't joyous – though it was loud.

Maybe you can't play a lick or carry a tune in the proverbial bucket. Or perhaps you do know your way around a guitar or a keyboard and can sing "Ramblin' Wreck" on karaoke night without closing the joint down. But unless you're a professional musician, how well you play or sing really doesn't matter. What counts is that you have music in your heart and sometimes you have to turn it loose – especially when the Yellow Jackets score and the Tech band plays.

That same boisterous and noisy enthusiasm should also be a part of the joy you have in your worship of God. Making "a joyful noise" to the Lord means just that, busting out in a racket for God. When you consider that God loves you and always will, how can you help but shout, holler, and sing – or even whisper -- your love in return?

I like it because it plays old music.
-- Pitcher Tug McGraw on his '54 Buick

You call it music; others may call it noise.
If it's joyful, send some God's way.

MIRACLE PLAYS

Read Matthew 12:38-42.

"He answered, 'A wicked and adulterous generation asks for a miraculous sign!'" (v. 39)

Georgia Tech had fallen victim to a miraculous comeback by Georgia in the 1997 game; in 1998, though, the Jackets proved miracles work both ways.

Both teams sported 8-2 records when they met in Athens on Nov. 28. Let by quarterback Joe Hamilton, the Jackets averaged 37 points per game; Tech's wins included UNC, Virginia, Clemson, and Maryland.

Tech's first score was exciting enough, though the Jackets had to do it twice. Georgia led 7-0 early in the second quarter when Charlie Rogers returned a punt 65 yards for an apparent touchdown. The refs ruled he had signaled a fair catch, though, and brought the ball back. Never mind. On the first play, Hamilton dropped a bomb to Kelly Campbell for a touchdown.

After that, though, the game seemed to belong to the Bulldogs. They took a 19-7 lead into the fourth quarter. As it turned out, a missed two-point conversion would be crucial.

Hamilton had the Jackets moving as the last period began. Joe Burns scored from ten yards out to complete a 62-yard, 12-play drive, and Hamilton scored the two-point conversion to put Tech right back in the game at 19-15.

A short drive yielded a clutch 49-yard Brad Chambers field

goal. That score came with only five minutes left, and it seemed any comeback would come up short. But the Jackets got one last possession, and with two seconds left, Chambers booted a 35-yard field goal to propel Tech to a miraculous 21-19 win. The Jackets had outscored Georgia 14-0 in the fourth quarter.

Miracles defy rational explanation – like three fourth-quarter scores to pull off a miraculous comeback. Or escaping with minor abrasions from an accident that totals your car. Or recovering from an illness that seemed terminal. Underlying the notion of miracles is that they are rare instances of direct divine intervention that reveal God.

But life shows us quite the contrary, that miracles are anything but rare. Since God made the world and everything in it, everything around you is miraculous. Even you are a miracle. Your life can be mundane, dull, and ordinary, or it can be spent in a glorious attitude of childlike wonder and awe. It depends on whether or not you see the world through the eyes of faith; only through faith can you discern the hand of God in any event. Only through faith can you see the miraculous and thus see God.

Jesus knew that miracles don't produce faith, but rather faith produces miracles.

Do you believe in miracles? Yes!
-- Broadcaster Al Michaels when U.S. defeated USSR in hockey in 1980
Winter Games

Miracles are all around us, but it takes the eyes
of faith to see them.

PROMISES, PROMISES

Read 2 Corinthians 1:16-20.

"No matter how many promises God has made, they are 'Yes' in Christ" (v. 20).

Brian Oliver promised his mother.

Oliver is one of the greatest basketball players in Georgia Tech history, a four-year starter and a member of the Hall of Fame. He is a two-time All America and the eighth leading scorer in Yellow Jacket roundball history.

The Jackets had finished the 1989-90 season at 21-6, third in the ACC. Oliver was one of three players – along with Dennis Scott and Kenny Anderson – who had averaged more than twenty points per game.

So Oliver, the team captain, was feeling pretty good about Tech's chances as the ACC Tournament approached. In an idle conversation with his mother, he said this year would be different for the Jackets. This time, Oliver said, "I'm going to bring a net back to you."

The promise didn't seem unreasonable under the circumstances, but Tech had a recent history then of doing little or nothing in the conference tournament. Since Oliver's arrival on campus in 1986, in fact, the Jackets had not won a single game in the tournament.

The 1990 tournament, of course, is part of Tech lore. The Jackets dispatched North Carolina State, Duke, and Virginia to claim the conference championship and begin the run to the Final Four.

Oliver won the tournament MVP award, and the team presented him with a net, which he wore around his neck even after he was fully dressed and had left the locker room. He had one more thing to do to complete his day: deliver that net to his momma. After all, he had promised.

The promises you make don't say much about you, but the promises you keep tell everything.

The promise to your daughter to be there for her softball game. To your son to help him with his math homework. To your parents to come see them soon. To your spouse to remain faithful until death parts you. And remember what you promised God?

You may carelessly throw promises around, but you can never outpromise God, who is downright profligate with his promises. For instance, he has promised to love you always, to forgive you no matter what you do, and to prepare a place for you with him in heaven.

And there's more good news in that God operates on this simple premise: Promises made are promises kept. You can rely absolutely on God's promises. The people to whom you make them should be able to rely just as surely on your promises.

In the everyday pressures of life, I have learned that God's promises are true.

-- *Major leaguer Garret Anderson*

God keeps his promises just as those who rely on you expect you to keep yours.

DAY 29

FATHERS AND SONS

Read Matthew 3:13-17.

"A voice from heaven said, 'This is my Son, whom I love; with him I am well pleased'" (v. 17).

As close as they were, Bobby Dodd Sr. and Bobby Dodd Jr. at one time came to a parting of the ways.

In the late 1950s, Dodd Jr. was quite a high school quarterback, which caused some agonizing in the Dodd household. Should the son play for the father at Tech? The two decided that such a situation wouldn't be fair to either of them. Coach Dodd explained his reasoning by outlining some possible situations: The son was a great college player and played, no problem; the son was a lousy college player and didn't play, no problem. The third scenario was the one fraught with problems. "Headaches come when [Bobby Jr.] is in the area in-between. Both Bobby and I agree he should play elsewhere," Tech's head man said.

The son eventually had a hand in dealing his dad a tough defeat. The Jackets were 2-0 when they arrived in Gainesville on Oct. 1, 1960, to meet the Gators and their alternating quarterbacks, Larry Libertore and Bobby Dodd Jr.

Asked before the game whether she would root for her husband's team or her son's team, Alice Dodd replied, "I hope Bobby Jr. has a fine day, and I hope Tech beats the devil out of them."

She got her first wish but not the second. A 32-yard Dodd Jr.

pass salvaged a late Florida drive that ended in a touchdown, a two-point conversion, and an 18-17 Gator win.

Al Thomy wrote, "The Dodds did not know whether to pat Bobby Jr. on the pads or cry."

American society largely belittles and marginalizes fathers and their influence upon their sons. Men are perceived as necessary to effect birth; after that, they can leave and everybody's better off.

But we need look in only two places to appreciate the enormity of that misconception: our jails – packed with males who lacked the influence of fathers in their lives as they grew up -- and the Bible. God – being God – could have chosen any relationship he desired between Jesus and himself, including society's approach of irrelevancy. Instead, the most important relationship in all of history was that of father-son. God obviously believes a close, loving relationship between fathers and sons, such as that of the Dodd men, is crucial. For men and women to espouse otherwise or for men to walk blithely and carelessly out of their children's lives constitutes disobedience to the divine will.

Simply put, God loves fathers. After all, he is one.

My dad was a huge influence on me. I imagine if he had put a wrench in my hand I would have been a great mechanic.

-- Pete Maravich

**Fatherhood is a tough job, but a model
for the father-child relationship is found
in that of Jesus the Son with God the Father.**

DAY 30

TOWEL THROWERS

Read Numbers 13:25-14:4.

"The men who had gone up with him said, 'We can't attack those people; they are stronger than we are'" (v. 13:31).

Kevin Tisdel had already called his parents and told them he was quitting Tech football. Had he followed through and left the team, the Jackets may well have missed out on the 1990 national championship.

Tisdel was a walk-on sophomore when he went to Coach Bobby Ross the week of the Clemson game and asked for a chance to return kickoffs. Ross agreed and put Tisdale into the game as the deep return man with Tech clinging to a 14-12 lead. Tisdel fielded the kickoff in the end zone, started up the left side, and sprinted to the Clemson 13, his 87-yard return setting up the game-winning touchdown in Tech's 21-19 win.

Two weeks later, to his dismay, Tisdel was not on the dress list for the Duke game. Distraught and disappointed, Tisdel told his parents he was through. In the locker room, sophomore nose guard Kevin Battle recommended that Tisdel talk to Ross before he did anything.

Ross immediately noticed Tisdel's long face, and when the player explained why, "Ross was as perplexed as the player was upset." Ross had inadvertently pulled out an old dress list that didn't include Tisdel. Ross assured Tisdel that not only was he dressing out for the Duke game, he was returning kickoffs.

Tech led only 24-21 late in the third quarter, its season in jeopardy, when Tisdel returned a kickoff 85 yards for a touchdown, breaking seven tackles and Duke's back in the process. In his post-game conference, Ross announced that Kevin Tisdel – who had been determined to quit – now had a scholarship.

Remember that time you quit a high-school sports team? Bailed out of a relationship? Walked away from that job with the goals unachieved? Sometimes quitting is the most sensible way to minimize your losses, so you may well at times in your life give up on something or someone.

In your relationship with God, however, you should remember the people of Israel, who quit when the Promised Land was theirs for the taking. They forgot one fact of life you never should: God never gives up on you.

That means you should never, ever give up on God. No matter how tired or discouraged you get, no matter that it seems your prayers aren't getting through to God, no matter what – quitting on God is not an option. He is preparing a blessing for you, and in his time, he will bring it to fruition -- if you don't quit on him.

Once you learn to quit, it becomes a habit.

– Vince Lombardi

Whatever else you give up on in your life, don't give up on God; he will never ever give up on you.

LEGAL THIEVERY

Read Exodus 22:1-15.

"A thief must certainly make restitution" (v. 2b).

Apparently nobody ever bothered to tell the Georgia Tech women's basketball team of 2007-08 that stealing is against the law.

The Jackets finished with a 22-10 record, the most victories since the school joined the ACC before the 1979-80 season. They earned a second straight bid to the NCAA Tournament.

The team had some offensive firepower. Senior Chioma Nnamaka, for instance, finished her career as the most prolific three-point shooter in Tech history. She and Janie Mitchell both passed the 1,000-point mark for a career during the season.

The team was the best in the nation, though, at the fine art of thievery. The Jackets averaged a jaw-dropping 14.3 steals per game to lead the country. Foremost among the pickpockets was junior Jacqua Williams, who set a school record for a season with 118 steals. Coach MaChelle Joseph said Williams' chief asset was her long arms. "She's 5-[foot]-6 with a 6-2 wingspan," the coach said. Williams, incidentally, was the hero in Tech's first-ever win in the NCAA Tournament in 2007. Nnamaka pulled down a rebound and passed to Williams, who drove for a layup that gave Tech a 55-54 win over DePaul.

Williams had plenty of help, though, in senior Jill Ingram. In

2007-08, Ingram had 101 steals, which would have been a school record for the season had Williams not been around. The season left Ingram third on the all-time steals list at the time. Williams would set a new school record for steals on Nov. 22, 2008, with her 279th career theft in a win over Mississippi Valley State.

Buckle up your seat belt. Wear a bicycle or motorcycle helmet. Use your pooper scooper to clean up after your dog. Don't walk on the grass. Nitpicky ordinances, nitpicky laws – in all their great abundance, they're an inescapable part of our modern lives.

When Moses came stumbling down Mt. Sinai after spending time as God's secretary, he brought with him a whole mess of laws and regulations, many of which seem as nitpicky as many of our contemporary legislative decrees. What some of them provide, though, are practical examples of what for God is the basic principle underlying the theft of personal property: what is wrong must be made right.

While most of us today probably won't have to worry too much about oxen, sheep, and donkeys, making what is wrong right remains a way of life for Christians. To get right with other people requires anything from restitution to apologies. To get right with God requires Jesus Christ.

When we played softball, I'd steal second base, feel guilty, and go back.
-- Woody Allen

To make right the wrong of stealing requires restitution; to make right our relationship with God requires Jesus Christ.

DAY 32

PAYBACK

Read Matthew 5: 38-42.

*"I tell you, Do not resist an evil person. If someone strikes
you on the right cheek, turn to him the other also" (v. 39).*

Many of those who gathered at Grant Field on Nov. 17, 1962,
for the Alabama game expected a bloodbath. It never happened
-- but the Jackets still got their revenge.

In the 1961 game in Birmingham, an Alabama player smashed
Tech's Chick Graning in the face "in an unnecessary block when
an Alabama teammate signaled for a fair catch on a punt." The
cheap shot came after the catch, "though possibly before the
referee's whistle had sounded." Graning had to be helped off the
field with serious injuries.

Tech fans, faculty, and alumni argued the injury was the
result of "a deliberate and brutal foul," calling it characteristic of
Alabama football. Coach Bobby Dodd had for some time sought
to drop Alabama from the Tech schedule, and so in January 1962,
the schools severed football relations after the 1964 game.

Thus, tension was high in 1962 with fans expecting Tech to
seek revenge for the injury and Alabama seeking to avenge the
insult. Instead, the game was well played with Dodd asking Bear
Bryant afterwards, "I believe that was the cleanest game I've ever
seen. What do you think, Coach?" Bryant agreed and added, "I
didn't except anything different."

What Bryant didn't expect was the final score. The Tide was

ranked No. 1 and unbeaten in 27 games, but Tech got an interception from Mike McNames, who returned it to the Alabama 16 and then scored two plays later. Alabama scored in the fourth quarter and failed on a two-point conversion try.

Tech had a 7-6 upset – and its revenge.

Somebody's done you wrong: that driver who cut you off, a coworker who lied about you to the supervisor, your ex who cheated on you. Time to get even? Of course, it is. What goes around comes around, buddy.

Hold on a minute, though. There's this little matter of Jesus' command not to seek revenge for wrongs and injuries. What we have here is an irreconcilable conflict between how the world says we should act and how God says we are to conduct ourselves.

And consider this: Resentment and anger hurt you and no one else. You're stewing in your own juices, poisoning your own happiness while that other person goes blithely on. The only way someone who has hurt you can keep hurting you is if you're a willing participant.

Jesus ushered in a new way of living when he taught that we are not to seek revenge for wrongs and injuries. What a relief!

I think football would become an even better game if someone could invent a ball that kicks back.

-- *Comedian Eric Morecambe*

Resentment and anger over a wrong injures you,
not the other person, so forget it --
just as Jesus taught.

DAY 33

THE SURE FOUNDATION

Read Luke 6:46-49.

"I will show you what he is like who comes to me and hears my words and puts them into practice. He is like a man building a house, who dug down deep and laid the foundation on rock" (vv. 47-48).

Perhaps no one in the . . . history of ACC basketball ranks as a greater program builder." So wrote Barry Jacobs about Bobby Cremins, but the Tech coach knew that building anything, including a national contender, requires a solid foundation. He found it in John Salley and Mark Price.

"I've got to give those two the credit for starting the program," Cremins said. "They are two very, very special people." They arrived in 1982. Bruce Dalrymple and Duane Ferrell came later, but "by then the Salley-Price alliance had come to symbolize Tech basketball." By the time they left in 1986, the foundation for greatness had been laid. Their legacy included two 27-win seasons, an ACC championship in 1985, trips to the Elite Eight in 1985 and the Sweet Sixteen in 1986 in the NCAA Tournament, and a No. 1 ranking during the 1985-86 season.

They could not have been more different, Price the shooting guard from Oklahoma and Salley the big man from Brooklyn. They met for the first time when Salley arrived on campus and rushed into Price's room in the middle of the night. He woke Price up to introduce himself "and nearly dropped from shock when a little Caucasian with droopy eyes sat up in his bed." "This little white dude's shootin' it 25 times a game?" Sally asked. They were the two, though "who rode shotgun during Tech's return to grace."

They remain two of Tech's greatest players, members of the Georgia Tech Hall of Fame with their jersey numbers retired.

Like Georgia Tech's entire athletic program, your life is an ongoing project, a work in progress. As with any complex construction job, if your life is to be stable, it must have a solid foundation, which holds everything up and keeps everything together.

R. Alan Culpepper said in *The New Interpreter's Bible*, "We do not choose whether we will face severe storms in life; we only get to choose the foundation on which we will stand." In other words, tough times are inevitable. If your foundation isn't rock-solid, you will have nothing on which to stand as those storms buffet you, nothing to keep your life from flying apart into a cycle of disappointment and destruction.

But when the foundation is solid and sure, you can take the blows, stand strong, recover, and live with joy and hope. Only one foundation is sure and foolproof: Jesus Christ. Everything else you build upon will fail you.

When I was younger, I thought that the key to success was just hard work. But the real foundation is faith.

-- Former NFL player Howard Twilley

In the building of your life, you must start with a foundation in Jesus Christ, or the first trouble that shows up will knock you down.

DAY 34

THE GRUDGE

Read Matthew 6:7-15.

"If you forgive men when they sin against you, your heavenly Father will also forgive you. But if you do not forgive men their sins, your Father will not forgive your sins" (vv. 14-15).

The most famous score in college football history probably came about because of a grudge.

Several factors played into Georgia Tech's 222-0 defeat of Cumberland on Oct. 7, 1916, but John Heisman, Tech's legendary and eccentric coach, almost certainly ran up the score as payback. Heisman insisted he broke his own rules about sportsmanship to shame the pollsters, who then as they do today, were often more impressed with blowouts against inferior competition than they were with close wins over strong opponents. But anymore who knew the situation, including the press and Tech fans, knew the truth.

Heisman had held a grudge against the Tennessee school since Cumberland had defeated the coach's baseball team 22-0 the previous spring. He learned some time after the game that the Cumberland coach, a law student named George Allen, had recruited professional players from Nashville. Allen wanted a convincing win over Tech to save the Cumberland athletic program from being disbanded by the school president.

The prideful Heisman didn't forget it, and Allen's scheme

didn't work as the Cumberland boss folded the athletic program, including the football team. The school informed Heisman of the situation, but still holding a grudge, the coach replied that if Cumberland didn't show up to play the football game he would sue the school for $3,000 for lost gate receipts.

Allen feared a lawsuit would doom any chances of saving athletics at Cumberland, so he persuaded some of his law-school buddies to play the game. They subsequently played their way into college football history.

It's probably pretty easy for you to recall times when somebody did you wrong. Have you held insistently onto your grudges so that the memory of each injury still drives up your blood pressure? Or have you forgiven that other person for what he or she did to you and shrugged it off as a lesson learned?

Jesus said to forgive others, which is exactly the sort of thing he would say. Extending forgiveness, though, is monumentally easier said than done. But here's the interesting part: You are to forgive for your sake, not for the one who injured you. When you forgive, the damage is over and done with. You can move on with your life, leaving the pain behind. The past – and that person -- no longer has power over you.

Holding a grudge is a way to self-destruction. Forgiving and forgetting is a way of life – a godly life.

You're doing all right, but you just can't tell what those Cumberland players have up their sleeves.
                    -- John Heisman to his players at halftime; Tech led 126-0

**Forgiving others frees you from your past,
turning you loose to get on with your life.**

FOOD FOR THOUGHT

Read Genesis 9:1-7.

"Everything that lives and moves will be food for you. Just as I gave you the green plants, I now give you everything"
(v. 3).

If you think you struggle with what you eat, just imagine being responsible for the dietary habits of the Georgia Tech football and basketball teams.

Dietician Roy Skinner had that job, and he faced a different situation for each athlete. For instance, defensive end Darrell Robertson (2004-07) had to gain weight and shed his nickname "Stick." "Eat everything in sight and keep working out" was Robertson's plan.

Receiver Kelly Campbell broke his jaw in the 1999 game against Florida State. His jaw was wired shut, so Skinner faced the problem of keeping Campbell's weight up. "He and I met for every single meal . . . and I liquefied every single meal for him," Skinner said.

Skinner also had the problem of weight maintenance for basketball forward Isma'il Muhammad. He was a practicing Muslim who did not eat or drink during the daylight hours of Ramadan, which in 2001, matched up with the early part of basketball season. Skinner got exact sunrise/sunset times from the Naval Observatory, and at precisely that time Muhammad would get a break from practice and be offered the traditional water and dates to break his fast.

Other food problems abound. The dining hall manager doesn't serve food with poppy seeds for fear of producing false positives on drug tests. Because of NCAA limits, athletes can't get a free bagel or fruit after practice, but they can get a free energy bar since it's classified as a supplement and not a food.

And you thought you had problems with your diet!

Belly up to the buffet, boys and girls, for barbecue, sirloin steak, grilled chicken, and fried catfish with hush puppies. Rachael Ray's a household name; hamburger joints, pizza parlors, and taco stands lurk on every corner; and we have a TV channel devoted exclusively to food. We love our chow.

Food is one of God's really good ideas, but consider the complex divine plan that gets those French fries to your mouth. The creator of all life devised a system in which living things are sustained and nourished physically through the sacrifice of other living things in a way similar to what Christ underwent to save you spiritually. Whether it's fast food or home-cooked, everything you eat is a gift from God secured through a divine plan in which some plants and animals have given up their lives.

Pausing to give thanks before you dive in seems the least you can do.

I cut down to six means a day.

-- Charles Barkley on losing weight

**God created a system that nourishes you
through the sacrifice of other living things;
that's worth a thank-you.**

THE UNEXPECTED

Read Luke 2:1-20.

"She gave birth to her firstborn, a son. She wrapped him in cloths and placed him in a manger, because there was no room for them in the inn" (v. 7).

That Georgia Tech would shock Kentucky on Jan. 8, 1955, and end the Wildcats' 129-game home winning streak was completely unexpected. Even more so was the player who was pivotal in the 59-58 win.

Bobby Kimmel hadn't even expected to be on the team. In the fall of 1953, Tech coach Whack Hyder got one of those unexpected phone calls that yield phenomenal dividends. The high school coach on the line told Hyder that Kimmel was in school at Tech and probably could help the team. Hyder followed up with the registrar's office and found that Kimmel was indeed in school. With nothing to lose, the coach dropped by Kimmel's dorm room. Kimmel was out, so Hyder left a note on the door telling Kimmel to come see him if he was interested in playing basketball. Kimmel had previously decided that he would not play college basketball, but he went by to see Hyder and the coach changed his mind. The following quarter he was on scholarship.

He made Yellow Jacket history in the Kentucky game. With 1:12 left, Kimmel, a 6-3 forward, hit two free throws to pull Tech to within one. On Kentucky's subsequent possession, he forced a turnover that gave the Jackets the chance to hit the game-winning shot.

Kimmel actually had a stand-out career with the Jackets. He led the team in scoring as a junior and was third-team All-ACC in 1956 and '57. He was the first-ever three-time team captain.

Bobby Kimmel's whole collegiate basketball career was totally unexpected – even by him.

Just like Bobby Kimmel and Whack Hyder, we think we've got everything figured out and planned for, and then something unexpected like a phone call happens to change everything. Someone gets ill; you fall in love; you lose your job; you're going to have another child. Life surprises us with its bizarre twists and turns.

God is that way too, catching us unawares to remind us he's still around. A friend who hears you're down and stops by, a child's laugh, an achingly beautiful sunset -- unexpected moments of love and beauty. God is like that, always doing something in our lives we didn't expect.

But why shouldn't he? There is nothing God can't do. The only factor limiting what God can do is the paucity of our own faith.

Expect the unexpected from God, this same deity who unexpectedly came to live among us as a man. He does, by the way, expect a response from you.

I had a good alibi ready. Then those crazy guys go out and win the game.
– Bobby Bowden after beating Cincinnati in 1979

God does the unexpected to remind you of his presence -- like showing up as Jesus – and now he expects a response from you.

DAY 37

ONE TOUGH COOKIE

Read 2 Corinthians 11:21b-29.

"Besides everything else, I face daily the pressure of my concern for all the churches" (v. 28).

The Yellow Jackets lost to Pittsburgh in 1920, but everyone – including the Eastern newspapers, which traditionally treated Southern football with disdain – praised the toughness of Tech's Red Barron.

1920 was Bill Alexander's first year at the helm, replacing the legendary John Heisman. Not much of a talker, Alexander's speech to his team before the season-opening game against Wake Forest consisted of one sentence: "It would be good to start off with a win." Tech won 44-0.

The Jackets then rolled over Oglethorpe 55-0, Davidson 66-0, and Vanderbilt 44-0. In the Vandy game, David Irenus Barron, "a runner of power and speed," suffered a broken jaw. Barron showed just how tough he was, though, because he had his jaw wired and played at least fifty minutes in each of the next four games.

That included the Pittsburgh game the week after Vandy. Buck Flowers drop-kicked an 18-yard field goal to give Tech a 3-0 lead "in the light snow of the Steel City," but Pitt rallied to win 10-3. The talk – even in Pittsburgh – was all about Barron's play with his teeth "fastened together with fine gold wires. He played on the strength of 12 chickens consumed in soup during the three days prior to the game." That was the only solid food Barron had consumed since his injury the Saturday before.

But Barron wasn't through demonstrating his toughness. When he returned to Atlanta, "his teeth were lashed by passing wires through his gums. It was a painful operation which Red underwent without anaesthetic."

Red Barron was one tough cookie.

You don't have to be a legendary Georgia Tech running back to be tough. In America today, toughness isn't restricted just to physical accomplishments and brute strength. Going to work every morning even when you feel bad, sticking by your rules for your children in a society that ridicules parental authority, making hard decisions about your aging parents' care often over their objections — you've got to be tough every day just to live honorably, decently, and justly.

Living faithfully requires toughness, too, though in America chances are you won't be imprisoned, stoned, or flogged this week for your faith as Paul was. Still, contemporary society exerts subtle, psychological, daily pressures on you to turn your back on your faith and your values. Popular culture promotes promiscuity, atheism, and gutter language; your children's schools have kicked God out; the corporate culture advocates amorality before the shrine of the almighty dollar.

You have to hang tough to keep the faith.

Winning isn't imperative, but getting tougher in the fourth quarter is.
-- Bear Bryant

Life demands more than mere physical toughness;
you must be spiritually tough too.

DAY 38

SMART MOVE

Read 1 Kings 4:29-34; 10:23-11:4.

"King Solomon was greater in riches and wisdom than all the other kings of the earth. The whole world sought audience with Solomon to hear the wisdom God had put in his heart" (vv. 10:23-24).

Coach George O'Leary made a smart move, and the result was an overtime win over Georgia.

The 1999 regular-season finale was one of the most exciting in the history of the series, a shootout from start to finish that ended tied at 48. Georgia had possession first in the overtime, and Marvious Hester intercepted a pass to give the Jackets a chance to win with a field goal. That's when O'Leary made his smart move.

In the radio announcing booth, color analyst Kim King knew what he would do as Tech faced third down: "You run one more play, don't do anything fancy, maybe run off tackle and get another four, five yards closer." It made sense; another four or five yards would make the game-winning field goal that much easier.

But O'Leary was thinking otherwise. He called for the field goal on third down. To the horror of Tech fans everywhere, the kick was blocked. But holder George Godsey had the presence of mind to recover the ball and get down to the Georgia 21. Now the brilliance of O'Leary's decision became apparent. Had the Jackets waited until fourth down and had the kick blocked, the ball would have been Georgia's and the game would continue.

Since the Jackets had kicked on third down, though, and had recovered the ball, they now had fourth down to attempt another kick.

This time Luke Manget got the kick off, and it was good for the 51-48 Tech win.

Smart move, coach.

Wouldn't it be nice if all our moves and decisions were as smart as O'Leary's? No matter how much formal education we have, though, we all make some dumb moves sometime because time spent in a classroom is not an accurate gauge of common sense. Folks impressed with their own smarts often grace us with erudite pronouncements that we intuitively recognize as flawed, unworkable, or simply wrong.

A good example is the observation that great intelligence and scholarship are not compatible with faith in God. That is, the more you know, the less you believe. But any incompatibility occurs only because we begin to trust in our own wisdom rather than the wisdom of God. We forget, as Solomon did, that God is the ultimate source of all our knowledge and wisdom and that even our ability to learn is a gift from God.

Not smart at all.

I don't hire anybody not brighter than I am. If they're not smarter than me, I don't need them.

-- Bear Bryant

Being truly smart means trusting in God's wisdom rather than only in your own knowledge.

DAY 39

JUMPING FOR JOY

Read Luke 6:20-26.

"Rejoice in that day and leap for joy, because great is your reward in heaven" (v. 23).

Chaunte Howard may well be the greatest jumper in Georgia Tech history – and it all started with a stick.

While she was at Tech, Howard won three straight national titles in the high jump: the 2004 NCAA Indoor Championships at which she set a new NCAA record, the 2004 NCAA Outdoor National Championships, and the 2005 Indoor National Championships, making her the first back-to-back national champion in Tech history. In 2004, she became the first Georgia Tech women's track and field athlete to qualify for the Olympics; in 2005 she became the first American woman to win a world outdoor championships medal in 22 years; and she was Olympic Trials champion in 2008.

The California native came east to work under Tech jumps coach Nat Page, who, she believed quite correctly, could help her achieve her dream of being an Olympian.

Howard noticed early on that she was athletic. In her elementary school, the teachers frequently made the children run around the softball and baseball fields, and Howard would always race the boys and beat them. Then starting in the third grade, "They started making us do mile time trials," and she was fast enough to decide then that she might be a pretty good athlete.

The next step came in middle school when she added jumping to her running. She remembered, "'I can jump over that stick' – and just challenging myself – 'Wow, I really CAN jump over the stick!'"

And Chaunte Howard kept jumping -- all the way into Tech athletic history.

You're probably a pretty good jumper yourself when Georgia Tech scores against Georgia, FSU, or Virginia Tech. You just can't help it. It's like your feet and your seat have suddenly become magnets that repel each other. The sad part is that you always come back down to earth; the moment of exultation passes.

But what if you could jump for joy all the time? Not literally, of course; you'd pass out from exhaustion. But figuratively, with your heart aglow and joyous even when life is its most difficult.

Joy is an absolutely essential component of the Christian life. Not only do we experience joy in our public praise and worship – which is temporary – but we live daily in the joy that comes from the quiet and sure confidence we have in God and his saving power extended to us through Jesus. This is a joy the tragedies and whims of the world can't touch.

No one can say 'You must not run faster than this, or jump higher than that.' The human spirit is indomitable.
-- Sir Roger Bannister, first to run a sub-4-minute mile

Unbridled joy can send you jumping all over the place; life in Jesus means such exultation is not rare but rather is a way of life.

DAY 40

AMAZING!

Read: Luke 4:31-36.

"All the people were amazed and said to each other, "What is this teaching? With authority and power he gives orders to evil spirits and they come out!"" (v. 36)

What Georgia Tech senior tailback Eddie Lee Ivery did on Nov. 11, 1978 – especially considering the circumstances -- was just downright amazing.

On 26 rushes against Air Force, Ivery rushed for 356 yards, the most in a single game by any back in college football history, leading the Jackets to a 42-21 win in absolutely horrible conditions. What the Jackets found as game-time neared was snow and a wind-chill factor of zero. "It was the coldest I'd ever been," quarterback Gary Lanier said.

The snow was so thick groundskeepers had to bring in street sweepers twice before kickoff. As he went out for warm-ups, Ivery thought conditions were so bad they wouldn't be able to play. A reporter described the field as so slick "ice skates would have been more appropriate footwear than cleated shoes."

Even if the teams played, Ivery wasn't sure he would play thanks to the plate of eggs he had for breakfast. The combination of eggs, freezing temperatures, and high altitude produced "a nausea omelet" in Ivery's stomach. He broke off a 73-yard touchdown run in the second quarter and promptly headed to the sideline to throw up.

At halftime, the trainers force-fed him Pepto-Bismol. As he neared the record of 350 yards in the fourth quarter, Ivery's stomach troubles returned, and he left the game. But Coach Pepper Rodgers put him back in, saying he'd let him run the ball every play until he got the record. Ivery eventually got it with a 21-yard run. His amazing line score was 356 yards and three touchdowns on 26 carries.

The word *amazing* defines the limits of what you believe to be plausible or usual. The Grand Canyon, the birth of your children, those last-second Yellow Jacket wins -- they're amazing! You've never seen anything like that before!

Some people in Galilee felt the same way when they encountered Jesus. Jesus amazed them with the authority of his teaching, and he wowed them with his power over spirit beings. People everywhere just couldn't quit talking about him.

It would have been amazing had they not been amazed. They were, after all, witnesses to the most amazing spectacle in the history of the world: God himself was right there among them walking, talking, teaching, preaching, and healing.

Their amazement should be a part of your life too because Jesus still lives. Almighty God seeks to spend time with you every day – because he loves you. Amazing!

It's amazing. Some of the greatest characteristics of being a winning football player are the same ones it's true to be a Christian man.
                                                              -- Bobby Bowden

Everything about God is amazing, but perhaps most amazing of all is that he loves us and desires our company.

DAY 41

DECIDE FOR YOURSELF

Read John 6:60-69.

"The words I have spoken to you are spirit and they are life. Yet there are some of you who do not believe" (vv. 63b-64a).

In 1964, Bobby Dodd made a decision that forever altered the landscape of Georgia Tech athletics; he pulled Tech out of the Southeastern Conference.

Tech helped form the SEC in 1933. Over the years, the Jackets won five SEC football championships, the last in 1952. Tech was thus a fixture in the conference. Dodd had chafed, however, at the conference's "140 Rule," which allowed member schools to put 140 football and basketball players on scholarship at one time. Since the schools generally carried fewer than fifteen scholarshipped basketball players, the football team could carry 125 to 130 players.

Dodd felt the rule left Tech at a competitive disadvantage. Unlike other coaches in the league, Dodd refused to run off unwanted players during the season just to meet the "140 rule." He believed the rule allowed schools to conduct "legal tryouts" of players and then dismiss from the team the ones who didn't make the grade.

Dodd sought to have the conference change the rule, convincing coaches and officials at five other SEC schools to vote with him to overturn it at the 1964 conference meeting. He even lobbied his old pal Bear Bryant to recommend a change to his president, and Bryant agreed to try. Alabama's president felt differently, however, and cast the first vote in the meeting to support the rule. Tech's president, Edwin Harrison, immediately announced Tech's withdrawal from the SEC.

Following the decision, the Jackets competed as an independent for fifteen years before joining the Atlantic Coast Conference in 1979.

The decisions you made along the way shaped your life at every pivotal moment. Some decisions you made suddenly and frivolously; some you made carefully and deliberately; some were forced upon you. Perhaps decisions made for frivolous reasons have determined how your life unfolds, and you may have discovered that some of those spur-of-the-moment decisions have turned out better than your carefully considered ones.

Of all your life's decisions, however, none is more important than one you cannot ignore: What have you done with Jesus? Even in his time, people chose to follow Jesus or to reject him, and nothing has changed; the decision must still be made and nobody can make it for you. Carefully considered or spontaneous – how you arrive at a decision for Jesus doesn't matter; all that matters is that you get there.

If you make a decision that you think is the proper one at the time, then that's the correct decision.
-- John Wooden

A decision for Jesus may be spontaneous or considered; what counts is that you make it.

THE BAD TIMES

Read Philippians 1:3-14.

"What has happened to me has really served to advance the gospel. . . . Because of my chains, most of the brothers in the Lord have been encouraged to speak the word of God more courageously and fearlessly" (vv. 12, 14).

In a game against Florida State in 2004, the Jacket pitcher started his windup when suddenly third-baseman Mike Trapani called a time-out and vomited on the infield dirt before signaling his pitcher to continue. The bewildered FSU third-base coach asked Trapani what was going on. "It's just Tourette's," Trapani answered matter-of-factly.

Difficult times began in Trapani's life when he was diagnosed with Tourette's syndrome as a child. For him, the neurological disorder means involuntary, sudden movements, uncontrollable vocal sounds, and bouts of acid reflux.

When he was in high school, the vomiting got so bad his teachers set a trash can by his desk. In the on-deck circle, he would "involuntarily squint, roll his eyes, and then jerk his head from side to side."

But the disorder didn't get Trapani down. "The big man upstairs is going to pick somebody he figures could handle it," he said. "It'll be all right." Interestingly, his disorder never interfered with Trapani when he batted or fielded ground balls. "When you're focusing, you never do it," he said, referring to the involuntary movements. Trapani finished his career at Tech in 2006 with a .324 career average. He was a team captain his senior season and second-team All-ACC as a second baseman his junior season.

He once said that when his Tourette's gets bad, he tells himself, "It can only get better from here." He was right; doctors are optimistic that the syndrome will go into remission in Trapani's mid-30s. His bad times that he refused to give in to will yield to better times.

Loved ones die. You're downsized. Your biopsy looks cancerous or you're diagnosed with a neurological disorder. Your spouse could be having an affair. Hard, tragic times are as much a part of life as backaches and insomnia.

This applies to Christians too. Faith in Jesus Christ does not exempt anyone from pain. Jesus promises he will be there for us to lead us through the valleys; he never promises that we will not enter them.

The question therefore becomes how you handle the bad times. You can buckle to your knees in despair and cry, "Why me?" Or you can hit your knees in prayer and ask, "What do I do with this?" Setbacks and tragedies are opportunities to reveal and to develop true character and abiding faith. Your faithfulness -- not your skipping merrily along through life without pain -- is what reveals the depth of your love for God.

If I were to say, "God, why me?" about the bad things, then I should have said, "God, why me?" about the good things that happened in my life.

– Arthur Ashe

**Faithfulness to God requires faith even in --
especially in -- the bad times.**

DAY 43

TRAILBLAZER

Read Luke 5:1-11.

"So they pulled their boats up on shore, left everything and followed him" (v. 11).

In a roll call of Tech basketball greatness -- Mark Price, Rich Yunkus, Tico Brown, Brian Oliver, Dennis Scott, Kenny Anderson, John Salley, Travis Best, and so many others – they all stand on the shoulders of one who went before: Roger Kaiser.

In 1957, Tech Coach Whack Hyder pulled off the greatest coup in Tech basketball history by convincing Kaiser to leave the basketball hotbed that was Indiana for the basketball wasteland that was Atlanta. When Kaiser arrived in town, he discovered "you couldn't even find an outdoor court down here." At his first freshman game, "there wasn't anybody there. I was used to playing to a full gym. I said to myself, 'What in the world am I doing here?'"

But he stayed, and his junior season "was a landmark in Tech history." Averaging 22.5 points per game, Kaiser led the Jackets to a 22-6 mark and the school's first-ever invitation to the NCAA Tournament.

They didn't exactly sneak up on anybody, entering the tournament ranked eighth in the country and receiving a first-round bye. They drew Ohio University and trailed the whole game until Kaiser nailed a pair of free throws with only 4:55 left. Kaiser scored 16 of Tech's last 23 points as the Jackets won 57-54.

In the NCAA's final eight, Tech drew a legendary Ohio State team featuring Jerry Lucas and John Havlicek and lost, though the scrappy Jackets stayed close until late. Kaiser had 27 points and had blazed the trail for other great players to follow.

Going to a place in your life you've never been before – as Roger Kaiser did when he came to Atlanta -- requires a willingness to take risks and face uncertainty head-on. You've undoubtedly had your moments when your latent pioneer spirit manifested itself. That time you changed careers, ran a marathon, volunteered at a homeless shelter, learned Spanish, or went back to school.

While attempting new things invariably begets apprehension, the truth is that when life becomes too comfortable and too familiar, it gets boring. The same is true of God, who is downright dangerous because he calls us to be anything but comfortable as we serve him. He summons us to continuously blaze new trails in our faith life, to follow him no matter what. Stepping out on faith is risky all right, but the reward is a life of accomplishment, adventure, and joy that cannot be equaled anywhere else.

Life is an adventure. I wouldn't want to know what's going to happen next.

-- Bobby Bowden

Unsafe and downright dangerous, God calls us out of the place where we are comfortable to a life of adventure and trailblazing in his name.

DAY 44

CHANGELESS

Read Hebrews 13:5-16.

"Jesus Christ is the same yesterday and today and forever" (v. 8).

hat game is this?

The helmet was a piece of leather with cotton under it, so the players let their hair grow long for additional protection. The ball was the shape of a watermelon, too big to hold in your hand and pass. A nose guard was about the only protection a player had. A player might have shoulder pads and hip pads, but only if he provided them himself.

Hiding the ball under a jersey. A field-goal kicker using his helmet for a tee. Spectators rushing onto the field and getting in the players' way. Players dragging ball carriers forward. Linemen holding hands and jumping to the right or to the left just before a play began. Darkness forcing games to be called. Teams deciding upon the length of the game once they showed up.

What game is this?

This was the wild and woolly game of college football in its early days, the 1890s and the turn of the century. Georgia Tech was part of those beginnings, fielding an informal team in 1892 that was coached by a professor. Largely unregulated and unsophisticated with no forward pass, college football was then a game we would barely recognize today.

Thank goodness, we might well say. Given the symmetry, the

excitement, the passion, and the sheer spectacle that surround today's college game, few, if any, Georgia Tech fans would long for the days when handles were sewn into the uniforms of ball carriers to make them easier to toss.

Football has changed – but then again so has everything else. Computers and CDs, cell phones and George Foreman grills – they may not have even been around when you were sixteen. Think about how style, cars, and tax laws constantly change. Don't be too harsh on the world, though, because you've changed also. You've aged, gained or lost weight, gotten married, changed jobs, or relocated.

Have you ever found yourself bewildered by the rapid pace of change, casting about for something to hold on to that will always be the same, that you can use for an anchor for your life? Is there anything like that in this world?

Sadly, the answer's no. As football illustrates, all the things of this world change.

On the other hand, there's Jesus, who is the same today, the same forever, always dependable, always loving you. You can grab hold of Jesus and never let go.

Baseball is for the leisurely afternoons of summer and for the unchanging dreams.
-- *Writer Roger Kahn*

**In our ever-changing and bewildering world,
Jesus is the same forever; his love for you
will never change.**

DAY 45

KEEP YOUR SPIRIT UP

Read Hebrews 3:12-19.

"Exhort one another every day, as long as it is called 'today,' so that none of you may be hardened by the deceitfulness of sin" (v. 13 NRSV).

A defeat on the field or the court tests school spirit, even among the cheerleaders. But a loss deeper than any ever encountered in sports challenged the spirit of Tech cheerleading captain Shelly Piver and her sister and fellow cheerleader Nikki.

In a school dominated by males, they were a rarity. "I get on an elevator, and it's me and five guys," said Nikki, a sophomore in 2005. But they weren't a double; at one time, they were a triple because the one who blazed the trail as a cheerleader at Tech was older sister Leanna. She had no intentions of attending Tech. "Nothing but geeks go there," she whined as a senior in 1995. One overnight visit to the campus changed her mind.

But in November 1998, Leanna was driving to cheerleading practice when she was killed in a collision with a truck. In a twist of fate, her organs were used to save the life of a former cheerleader who had depended on her spirit to keep her going.

Both Shelly and Nikki tried out for Tech's cheerleading squad "to keep their sister's spirit alive." "I wanted to do something Leanna couldn't do. I want to finish it out," said Shelly, a senior in 2005.

The sisters know about rebounding spirit quickly. They sang at

Leanna's memorial the day after the funeral, and Shelly cheered at her high school's playoff game that weekend. Leanna's spirit lives on in the family's annual presentation of college scholarships for high-school cheerleaders.

For the Pivers, spirit is on their side.

You're exhausted, but your desk is stacked with work. And then suddenly your personal cheerleading team appears. They dance, cheer, shout, wave pompoms, and generally exhort you to more and greater effort. They fire you up. That would work, wouldn't it? If only . . .

But you do have just such a squad in your faith life: your fellow Christians. They come in teams -- called churches -- and they are exhorters who keep each other "in the game" that is faith.

Without the love, the support, and the encouragement of fellow believers, the Christian who spurns a church family is an easy target for indifference to creep into his life and separate him from his faith.

A church isn't really a building. It is, rather, a group of people who gather not just for worship and fellowship but also to exhort each other, to keep everyone's spirit up. Christians are cheerleaders for God -- and for God's team.

A good cheerleader is not measured by the height of her jumps but by the span of her spirit.

-- Source unknown

**In the people of your church,
you have your own set of cheerleaders
who urge you to greater faithfulness.**

DAY 46

ANIMAL MAGNETISM

Read Psalm 139:1-18.

"For you created my inmost being; you knit me together in my mother's womb. I praise you because I am fearfully and wonderfully made" (vv. 13-14).

One Tech player came back from the 1929 Rose Bowl with more than a national championship. He wound up with a bear.

Halfback Jack "Stumpy" Thomason was honorable mention All-America in 1928. He was a key part of the build-up for the game with California; his picture with movie star Alice White graced all the Atlanta papers.

After the game, fullback Roy "Father" Lumpkin turned pro and tried to take Thomason with him. Thomason considered the idea but then decided against it for two reasons: He wanted to get a degree and he had another mouth to feed. The mouth belonged to Bruin, a young brown bear given to the team by an Atlanta businessman in honor of the win over the California Bears. Thomason took on the chore of caring for Bruin.

That care included riding about Atlanta together and supplying Bruin with one of his favorite dietary staples: Coca-Cola. George Griffin, Tech's dean of students, said Bruin was "at least as smart as most Tech students, with all of the vices of modern youth."

Bruin resided under the east stands of Grant Field, often roaming the campus and raiding the trash cans of nearby homes. Atlanta police officers frequently received calls about the bear.

They would coax Bruin into the back of their squad car and escort him back to the Tech campus.

Eventually Bruin grew up, and his size made him something of a threat rather than a fun-filled nuisance, so Thomason donated him to the Buffalo, N.Y., zoo.

Animals such as Bruin elicit our awe and our respect. Nothing enlivens a trip more than glimpsing turkeys, bears, or deer in the wild. Admit it: You go along with the kids' trip to the zoo because you think it's a cool place too. All that variety of life is mind-boggling. Who could conceive of a walrus, a moose, or a prairie dog? Who could possibly have that rich an imagination?

But the next time you're at a Tech game, look around at the parade of faces. Who could come up with the idea for all those different people? For that matter, who could conceive of you? You are unique, a masterpiece who will never be duplicated.

The master creator, God Almighty, is behind it all. He thought of you and brought you into being. If you had a manufacturer's label, it might say, "Lovingly handmade in Heaven by #1 -- God."

That's just Stumpy's bear. Leave him alone and he'll go home.
– Atlanta police officer answering a call about a bear on a back porch

You may consider some painting a work of art,
but the real masterpiece is you.

DAY 47

NOT WHAT THEY SEEM

Read Habakkuk 1:2-11.

"Why do you make me look at injustice? Why do you tolerate wrong? Destruction and violence are before me; there is strife, and conflict abounds" (v. 3).

If you sat down with an old newspaper and perused the stats of the 1954 Georgia Tech-Georgia football game, you could rationally come to only one conclusion: Georgia beat the stew out of Tech. Ah, but in football quite often things are not what they seem.

The whole strategy and pace of the game was determined by the weather. A relentless downpour turned the Athens turf into mud and blasted fans with icy, wet winds.

Apparently, the conditions didn't bother Georgia. The Bull-dogs rolled up twelve first downs and 327 total yards to Tech's three and 73 respectively. The Jackets had six turnovers; Georgia had one. Moreover, Tech crossed the fifty-yard line only once the entire game.

So just what was the final score? Incredibly, Tech won 7-3 as Bobby Dodd coached one of his most brilliant games ever, adopting "the old Vol waiting game, kicking always on third down, taking nary a chance and waiting for a break."

Georgia led 3-0 at halftime. Tech didn't even have a first down and had 18 total yards, but the Jackets were grimly hanging on, waiting for that one break.

They got it on the first play of the second half when Franklin Brooks recovered a fumble at the Georgia 19. On the first play, quarterback Wade Mitchell hit Henry Hair with a strike in the end zone, Tech's only pass completion of the game. Mitchell added the extra point, and the final score was on the board.

Tech claimed a gritty win in a game in which every indicator said Georgia won.

Sometimes in life things aren't what they seem. In our violent and convulsive times, we must confront the possibility of a new reality: that we are helpless in the face of anarchy; that injustice, destruction, and violence are pandemic in and symptomatic of our modern age. It seems that anarchy is winning, that the system of standards, values, and institutions we have cherished is crumbling while we watch.

But we should not be deceived or disheartened. God is in fact the arch-enemy of chaos, the creator of order and goodness and the architect of all of history. God is in control. We often misinterpret history as the record of mankind's accomplishments -- which it isn't -- rather than the unfolding of God's plan -- which it is. That plan has a clearly defined end: God will make everything right. In that day things will be what they seem.

Unlike any other business in the United States, sports must preserve an illusion of perfect innocence.

-- Author Lewis H. Lapham

The forces of good and decency often seem helpless before evil's power, but don't be fooled: God is in control and will set things right.

TOLD YOU SO

Read Matthew 24:15-31.

"See, I have told you ahead of time" (v. 25).

Told you so," free safety Ken Swilling said to his head coach, Bobby Ross, after the 1990 Georgia game – and no words could have made Ross any happier.

The Jackets headed into 1990 coming off a seven-win season. For the most part, though, expectations for the season were tempered by realism. Ross, for instance, "had less lofty aims than many, hoping merely to win at least seven games," which would give Tech consecutive seven-win seasons for the first time since the Bobby Dodd era. Offensive coordinator Ralph Friedgen thought the team could win eight games "if things went right for us and we stayed healthy. I would have been very happy with a 7-4 season."

But that's not what Swilling had in mind. Inducted into the Georgia Tech Athletic Hall of Fame in 2000, Swilling was a consensus All-America in 1990 and first-team All-ACC in both 1989 and '90. He set the school record for tackles by a defensive back (267).

Swilling had no intentions of regarding a seven- or eight-win season as a success. On Tech's Media Day in August, a reporter asked Swilling for a prediction for the upcoming season. "11-0 would be an excellent record. And it's very feasible," Swilling replied. His prediction promptly drew raised eyebrows and a few snickers. Asked about Swilling's prognostication abilities, Ross, too, rolled his eyes and said, "That's a young man talking."

After Tech completed an undefeated season by gouging Georgia 40-23, Swilling couldn't resist a jab at his head coach: "Told you so."

Don't you just hate it in when somebody says, "I told you so"? That means the other person was right and you were wrong; that other person has spoken the truth. You could have listened to that know-it-all in the first place, but then you would have lost the chance yourself to crow, "I told you so."

In our pluralistic age and society, many view truth as relative, meaning absolute truth does not exist. All belief systems have equal value and merit. But this is a ghastly, dangerous fallacy because it ignores the truth that God proclaimed in the presence and words of Jesus.

In speaking the truth, Jesus told everybody exactly what he was going to do: come back and take his faithful with him. Those who don't listen or who don't believe will be left behind with those four awful words, "I told you so," ringing in their ears and wringing their souls.

There's nothing in this world more instinctively abhorrent to me than finding myself in agreement with my fellow humans.
-- Lou Holtz

Jesus matter-of-factly told us what he has planned:
He will return to gather all the faithful to himself.

HEAD GAMES

Read Job 28.

"The fear of the Lord -- that is wisdom, and to shun evil is understanding" (v. 28).

Thinking man that he is, Anthony McHenry didn't need too long to figure out that playing basketball in the Dakotas in the dead of winter was not how he wanted to spend his life.

Playing at Tech from 2001-05, McHenry averaged only 2.8 points and 2.3 rebounds per game. Yet, as a junior, he was a starting forward on and a vital part of the greatest team in Yellow Jacket basketball history: the 28-10 squad of 2003-04 that tied the school record for wins and advanced to the national championship game. He also started his senior season. If production wasn't the key to his value to the team, what was?

"He was the X factor," teammate Marvin Lewis said of him. As Coach Paul Hewitt put it, McHenry had "good basketball IQ." In fact, his nickname at Tech was "Q." "He understands the game both from an offensive and a defensive standpoint," Hewitt said. In short, McHenry was a "coach in waiting."

He realized that for sure after he joined the Fort Worth Flyers in the NBA Development League for the 2006-07 season and encountered the joys of a Dakota winter. "There was like two or three feet of snow everywhere," the Birmingham native said.

Always using his head, McHenry remembered that when he was a sophomore Hewitt had suggested he would make a good coach. So McHenry returned to Tech for the 2007-08 season, thinking things through as a student assistant, sitting one row behind the Yellow Jacket bench. He wasn't being paid but he was "soaking up knowledge."

You're a thinking person. When you talk about using your head, you're emulating Anthony McHenry in that logic and reason are part of your psyche, even if the game is basketball. A coach's bad call frustrates you and your children's inexplicable behavior flummoxes you. Why can't people just think things through?

That goes for matters of faith, too. Jesus doesn't tell you to turn your brain off when you walk into a church or open the Bible. In fact, when you seek Jesus, you seek him heart, soul, body, and mind. The mind of the master should be the master of your mind so that you consider every situation in your life through the critical lens of the mind of Christ. With your head *and* your heart, you encounter God, who is, after all, the true source of all knowledge and wisdom.

To know Jesus is not to stop thinking; it is to start thinking divinely.

Football is more mental than physical, no matter how it looks from the stands.
> -- *Pro Hall-of-Fame linebacker Ray Nitschke*

**Since God is the source of all wisdom,
it's only logical that you encounter him
with your mind as well as your emotions.**

DAY 50

THE BIG TIME

Read Matthew 2:19-23.

"He went and lived in a town called Nazareth" (v. 23).

He left his home in the Kentucky mountains in 1906 without a decent high-school education and wasn't good enough to make the football team at Tech. But he went on to become a college math instructor, the coach of a national championship team, and Georgia Tech's athletic director.

William Alexander had such a poor background that he needed six years to graduate from Tech. He also wasn't a very good college football player. One sportswriter said he wasn't blessed with size, speed, or talent. So he claimed a spot on John Heisman's "scrub" team, today's scout team, and eventually was named the scrubs' captain because "he's never absent, he's always trying, and he's always at the bottom of the pile."

He didn't even get to see the varsity play; he spent each Saturday scouting future opponents. Heisman so appreciated Alexander's efforts that he let him play in two games his senior year so he could letter. When he graduated, Alexander joined Heisman's staff and then succeeded him as head coach in 1920.

He led Tech's football fortunes through the 1944 season, succeeded by Bobby Dodd. Knute Rockne once remarked that Alexander got "more out of less than any coach in America." He won 134 games, including the 1928 national championship and

Tech's first three SEC titles. When he died in 1950 after 44 years of being associated with Georgia Tech, Alexander was still the athletic director.

Though he started back in the Kentucky mountains, William Alexander finished in the big time.

The move to the big time is one we often desire to make in our own lives. Bumps in the road, one stoplight communities, and towns with only a service station, a church, and a voting place litter the American countryside. Maybe you were born in one of them and grew up in a virtually unknown village in a backwater county. Perhaps you started out on a stage far removed from the bright lights of Broadway, the glitz of Hollywood, or the halls of power in Washington, D.C.

Those original circumstances don't have to define or limit you, though, for life is much more than geography. It is primarily about character and walking with God whether you're in the countryside or the city.

Jesus knew the truth of that. After all, he grew up in a small town in an inconsequential region of an insignificant country ruled by foreign invaders.

Where you are doesn't matter. What you are does.

I live so far out in the country that I have to walk toward town to go hunting.
-- Former major leaguer Rocky Bridges

**Where you live may largely be the culmination
of a series of circumstances; what you are
is a choice you make.**

HOMESICK

Read 2 Corinthians 5:1-10.

"We . . . would prefer to be away from the body and at home with the Lord" (v. 8).

Alexandra Preiss' sense of adventure took her all the way from Germany to Atlanta, but it couldn't keep her from suffering homesickness.

Preiss grew up in Nauheim, Germany, near Frankfurt. After high school, both Preiss and Georgia Tech took a chance. Tech signed her sight unseen to a volleyball scholarship, figuring a 6-foot-3 middle blocker on the German junior national team could help the Jackets. Preiss was looking for help, too. "I just wanted to improve as a volleyball player," she said.

What coaches Shelton Collier and Bond Shymansky got was one of the greatest players in Tech volleyball history who helped lift the program to new heights. By the time Preiss graduated in 2003, she was first-team All-ACC and honorable mention All-America. The two-time team captain set the school record for career hitting percentage and finished fifth all-time in career block assists, career total blocks, and career blocks per game, and ninth all-time in career kills.

Her senior season she led the team into the NCAA's Sweet 16 for the first time in school history – in Honolulu. The ACC champions set a school record for wins, finishing at 34-4.

Despite her success, Preiss struggled to adapt to life in the

United States. "It wouldn't have surprised me if she had stayed in Germany after her first season," Shymansky said.

She also was homesick for her family the whole time she was in Atlanta, and she returned to Germany after she graduated. Preiss admitted, though, in addition to her friends, she would miss one aspect of American life she couldn't find at home: Taco Bell.

Home is not necessarily a matter of geography. It may be that place you share with your spouse and your children, whether it's Germany or Atlanta. You may feel at home when you return to The Flats, wondering why you were so eager to leave in the first place. Maybe the home you grew up in still feels like an old shoe, a little worn but comfortable and inviting.

God planted that sense of home in us because he is a God of place, and our place is with him. Thus, we may live a few blocks away from our parents and grandparents or we may relocate every few years, but we still will sometimes feel as though we don't really belong no matter where we are. We don't; our true home is with God in the place Jesus has gone ahead to prepare for us. We are homebodies and we are perpetually homesick.

Everybody's better at home.

– Basketball player Justin Dentmon

**We are continually homesick for our real home,
which is with God in Heaven.**

SUCCESS STORY

Read Galatians 5:16-26.

"So I say, live by the Spirit. . . . The sinful nature desires what is contrary to the Spirit. . . . The acts of the sinful nature are obvious: . . . I warn you, as I did before, that those who live like this will not inherit the kingdom of God" (vv. 16, 17, 19, 21).

Within minutes of Georgia Tech's 79-71 overtime win over Kansas that earned a spot in the 2004 NCAA Final Four, Coach Paul Hewitt was sharing the success.

He called Dennis Scott and other members of the 1990 team, which gave Tech its first-ever trip to the Final Four. "Dennis, I want you in San Antonio [for the Final Four]," Hewitt said. "I want you to talk to the team." "I told Coach Hewitt I would be honored, and I can't wait to get there," Scott said. "Right now I feel like a kid in a candy store."

Hewitt also invited Bobby Cremins, his predecessor, to San Antonio. "I was a nervous wreck," Cremins said about watching the Kansas game in a downtown Atlanta restaurant after a speaking engagement. "I can't tell you how excited I am for Paul and for Georgia Tech."

Hewitt went on to invite other former Tech players and coaches, using up the allotment of 25 tickets set aside expressly for that purpose. Matt Harpring, Mark Price, Duane Ferrell, and Kenny Anderson – they were among the former players who made it to

San Antonio to watch Tech defeat Oklahoma State 67-65 in the semifinals before the most successful season in Yellow Jacket basketball history ended with a loss to Connecticut in the finals.

Hewitt understood that he couldn't build Tech's future without embracing the entire Georgia Tech basketball family. In pursuit of that goal, he did not hoard the 1994 team's success but shared it gladly with Tech's past.

Are you a successful person? Your answer, of course, depends upon how you define success. Is the measure of your success based on the number of digits in your bank balance, the square footage of your house, that title on your office door, the size of your boat?

Certainly the world determines success by wealth, fame, prestige, awards, and possessions. Our culture screams that life is all about gratifying your own needs and wants. If it feels good, do it. It's basically the Beach Boys' philosophy of life.

But all success of this type has one glaring shortcoming: You can't take it with you. Eventually, Daddy takes the T-bird away. Like life itself, all these things are fleeting.

A more lasting way to approach success is through the spiritual rather than the physical. The goal becomes not money or backslaps by sycophants but eternal life spent with God. Success of that kind is forever.

Success demands singleness of purpose.

-- Vince Lombardi

Success isn't permanent, and failure isn't fatal -- unless you're talking about your relationship with God.

DAY 53

THE FUNERAL

Read Romans 6:3-11.

"If we died with Christ, we believe that we will also live with him" (v. 8).

The toughest day of Billy Martin's life was the day he helped carry Billy Lothridge to his grave.

From the time when they were children and their families moved down the street from each other in Gainesville, Martin and Lothridge did everything together. They played football together, became Georgia Tech legends together, and even dated the same girls. Martin's wife was Lothridge's high-school sweetheart.

"Our dads decided we were going to Georgia Tech," Martin said. So they went off to Atlanta in 1960 as teammates and roommates, the tight end/linebacker and the quarterback/kicker. They flourished on The Flats. With freshmen ineligible to play varsity ball back then, Lothridge started at quarterback the third game of his sophomore season. He led Tech to a 21-10-1 record with appearances in the Gator and Bluebonnet bowls. He was All-SEC in 1962 and '63 and All-America in 1963. Martin was All-SEC and All-America in 1963. Also in 1963, Lothridge finished second to Navy quarterback Roger Staubach in the voting for the Heisman Trophy.

Lothridge and Martin went on to have professional careers, the draft separating them for the first time since they were children. They finished their pro careers together with the Falcons. Both were inducted into the Georgia Tech Hall of Fame.

They were inseparable – until Feb. 22, 1996, when Lothridge died of a heart attack. "We've done everything in our lives together," Martin said. "It just didn't occur to me he would ever be gone." Former teammates including Bill Curry and Tommy Nobis eulogized the Tech legend. Martin was among the pallbearers.

Chances are you won't get the kind of send-off that includes legendary sports figures such as Billy Martin, Bill Curry, and Tommy Nobis. Still, you want a good funeral. You want a decent crowd, you want folks to shed some tears, and you want some reasonably distinguished looking types to stand behind a lectern and say some very nice things about you. Especially if they're all true.

But have you ever been to a funeral where the deceased you knew and the deceased folks were talking about were two different people? Where everyone struggled to say something laudatory about the not-so-dearly-departed? Or a funeral that was little more than an empty acknowledgement that death is the end of all hope? Sad, isn't it?

Exactly what does make a good funeral, one where people laugh, love, and remember warmly and sincerely amid their tears? Jesus does. His presence transforms a mourning of death into a celebration of life.

Always go to other people's funerals; otherwise, they won't come to yours.

-- *Yogi Berra*

Amid tears there is hope; amid death there is resurrection – if Jesus is at the funeral.

DRY AS A BONE

Read John 4:1-25.

*"Everyone who drinks this water will be thirsty again,
but whoever drinks the water I give him will never thirst.
Indeed, the water I give him will become in him a spring
of water welling up to eternal life" (vv. 13-14).*

From 1949 through the 1956 season, Georgia Tech beat Georgia eight straight times, a stretch that is lamented in Bulldog lore and celebrated by Tech fans as "The Drought." The Jackets had quite a few drought makers during that remarkable stretch.

In 1949, Coach Bobby Dodd got the streak started when he opted for a quick kick in the fourth quarter with Georgia leading 6-0. The kick was downed at the Georgia five. Tech held and Georgia punted but only to the 39. Six plays later quarterback Jim Southard sneaked in from the one, and Tech won 7-6.

In 1950, the drought maker was senior right tackle Lamar Wheat. In a scoreless game, he recovered a Georgia fumble at the Tech 26. From there, Tech drove for the game's only touchdown on a run by Darrell Crawford.

Fullback George Maloof scored 24 points to pace the 48-6 Jacket win in 1951. The drought maker in 1952 was Chappell "One-Play" Rhino. (See devotion No. 79.)

Quarterback Pepper Rodgers threw for one touchdown and ran for another in the 28-6 blowout of Georgia in 1953.

After that, one player, quarterback Wade Mitchell, was three times the hero against Georgia. He threw the game-winning touchdown to Henry Hair in the 7-3 win in 1954 (See devotion No. 47.), made a touchdown-saving and momentum-swinging tackle in 1955, a 21-3 win, and ignited 1956's 35-0 blowout with a touchdown run.

Georgia Tech's drought makers were a big part of the glory years under Dodd.

You can walk across that river you boated on in the spring. The city's put all neighborhoods on water restriction, and that beautiful lawn you fertilized and seeded will turn a sickly, pale green and may lapse all the way to brown. Somebody wrote "Wash Me" on the rear window of your truck.

The sun bakes everything, including the concrete. The earth itself seems exhausted, just barely hanging on. It's a drought.

It's the way a soul looks that shuts God out.

God instilled thirst in us to warn us of our body's need for physical water. He also gave us a spiritual thirst that can be quenched only by his presence in our lives. Without God, we are like tumbleweeds, dried out and windblown, offering the illusion of life where there is only death.

Living water -- water of life -- is readily available in Jesus. We may drink our fill, and thus we slake our thirst and end our soul's drought -- forever.

Drink before you are thirsty. Rest before you are tired.
-- Paul de Vivie, father of French cycle touring

**Our souls thirst for the refreshing presence
of God.**

DAY 55

GOD'S WORKFORCE

Read Matthew 9:35-38

*"Then he said to his disciples, 'The harvest is plentiful but
the workers are few. Ask the Lord of the harvest, therefore,
to send out workers into his harvest field'" (vv. 37-38).*

In Paul Johnson's hometown of Newland, N.C., Santa Claus
sometimes shows up for the Christmas parade wearing bib over-
alls instead of a red suit. This says a great deal about the man
hired after the 2007 season to head up the Georgia Tech football
program.

Paul Johnson will never be outworked.

He rarely needs an alarm clock to get him up and running.
"There might be mornings I come in at 4 o'clock," he said about
getting to the office before his assistants do. "I can get more done
sometimes from 6 to 8 than I can from 8 to 1."

Johnson grew up working in a working town. He learned from
his dad to rise early and work hard. When he was 12, he hitch-
hiked to his job as a golf caddie.

Johnson took that obsession with hard work to Georgia
Southern where he won two consecutive Division 1-AA national
titles and to Navy where he coached the midshipmen to an
unprecedented five straight bowl games. He won 73 percent of
his games in Statesboro and Annapolis.

Johnson's impact on Georgia Tech football was immediate
and stunning. The Jackets had a breakout 9-3 season in 2008 that

included wins over Georgia and Florida State and a trip to the Chick-Fil-A Bowl. He was named the ACC Coach of the Year.

Taz Anderson, who captained Bobby Dodd's 1959 team, said Johnson was a perfect fit for Tech because "his offense allows a team to be decent if it plays smart." Working hard and playing smart – Paul Johnson's recipe for winning.

Do you embrace hard work or try to avoid it? No matter how hard you may try, you really can't escape hard work. Funny thing about all these labor-saving devices like cell phones and laptop computers: You're working longer and harder than ever.

For many of us, our work defines us perhaps more than any other aspect of our lives. But there's a workforce you're a part of that doesn't show up in any Labor Department statistics or any IRS records.

You're part of God's staff; God has a specific job that only you can do for him. It's often referred to as a "calling," but it amounts to your serving God where there is a need in the way that best suits your God-given abilities and talents

You should stand ready to work for God all the time, 24-7. Those are awful hours, but the benefits are out of this world.

I've always believed that if you put in the work, the results will come.
– Michael Jordan

God calls you to work for him using the talents and gifts he gave you; whether you're a worker or a malingerer is up to you.

DAY 56

GOOD SPORTS

Read Titus 2:1-8.

"Show integrity, seriousness and soundness of speech that cannot be condemned, so that those who oppose you may be ashamed because they have nothing bad to say about us" (vv. 7b, 8).

He was so good that when he left the floor for his last conference game, he elicited an unprecedented show of sportsmanship from his opponents' fans: They gave him a standing ovation.

From the moment he first stepped onto the court at Alexander Memorial Coliseum, Matt Harpring was something special. From 1994-98, he set the standard for work, determination, and all-out hustle. He even declined to turn pro after his junior season, saying he wanted to come back and "help get Tech basketball back where it belongs" after the Jackets had a disappointing 1996-97 season.

Harpring finished second in Tech history in both scoring and rebounding and finished among Tech's career leaders in virtually every category. His No. 15 jersey was retired prior to his final home game.

The ACC Tournament in 1998 provided a fitting ending to his wonderful college career. The Jackets lost to Maryland in the opening round of the tournament, and with just over a minute left, Coach Bobby Cremins called his All-American senior to the bench. As expected, the Tech crowd stood and cheered, but then something rare and special happened. "The applause spread to every corner of the 24,000-seat Greensboro Coliseum as fans wearing every shade of Carolina blue, NC State red and Clemson orange joined in." On the bench, a dejected Harpring did not realize what was happening until Cremins and his teammates coaxed him into waving to the crowd.

"I don't know why they did it," Harpring said. "But it was a huge honor and compliment."

And a show of sportsmanship from ACC fans.

One of life's paradoxes is that many who would never consider cheating on the tennis court or the racquetball court to gain an advantage think nothing of doing so in other areas of their life. In other words, the good sportsmanship they practice on the golf course or even on the Monopoly board doesn't carry over. They play with the truth, cut corners, abuse others verbally, run rough-shod over the weaker, and generally cheat whenever they can to gain an advantage on the job or in their personal relationships.

But good sportsmanship is a way of living, not just of playing. Shouldn't you accept defeat without complaint (You don't have to like it.); win gracefully without gloating; treat your competition with fairness, courtesy, generosity, and respect? That's the way one team treats another in the name of sportsmanship. That's the way one person treats another in the name of Jesus.

One person practicing sportsmanship is better than a hundred teaching it.
-- Knute Rockne

Sportsmanship -- treating others with courtesy, fairness, and respect -- is a way of living, not just a way of playing.

DAY 57

CLOCKWORK

Read Matthew 25:1-13.

"Keep watch, because you do not know the day or the hour" (v. 13).

Tech once employed a strategy against Georgia that left its fans dumbfounded and could have cost the Institute the game. The mistake resulted from confusion about how much time was left in the half.

Tech and Georgia had not met in football since 1916 when they renewed their rivalry on Nov. 14, 1925. Thirty-three thousand fans, the largest crowd ever to see a Southern football game, crammed Grant Field to watch 5-2 Tech do battle with 4-3 Georgia.

The Bulldogs recovered an early Tech fumble, but Tech's defense forced an errant field goal attempt. The two teams then slugged it out without either squad threatening to score until Tech mounted a threat late in the half. The Yellow Jackets moved to the Georgia six when captain Doug Wycoff, knowing halftime was near, asked the referee to see how much time was left before the intermission. The ref dutifully trotted to the timekeeper on the sideline, who informed him one minute and 15 seconds remained. The official, however, heard only the 15 seconds, and so informed Wycoff. Tech immediately attempted a field goal and missed it.

To the dismay of the Institute's team and its followers, the officials brought the ball out to the 20 from which Georgia ran four plays before the half ended. "The big crowd was dumb-founded.

114 DAY 57

What kind of crazy strategy had Tech employed?"

As it turned out, the mistake with the clock didn't affect the outcome. Ivan Williams' third-quarter field goal from the 35 stood up for a 3-0 Tech win.

We may pride ourselves on our time management, but the truth is that we don't manage time; it manages us. Hurried and harried, we live by schedules that seem to have too much what and too little when. By setting the bedside alarm at night, we even let the clock determine how much down time we get. A life of leisure actually means one in which time is of no importance.

Every second of our life – all the time we have – is a gift from God, who dreamed up time in the first place. We would do well, therefore, to ponder exactly what God considers to be good time management. After all, Jesus himself warned us against mismanaging the time we have. From God's point of view, using our time wisely means being prepared at every moment for Jesus' return, which will occur -- well, only time will tell when.

We didn't lose the game; we just ran out of time.

– Vince Lombardi

We mismanage our time when we fail to prepare for Jesus' return even though we don't know when that will be.

DAY 58

HOME IMPROVEMENT

Read Hebrews 6:1-12.

"Let us go on towards perfection" (v. 1 NRSV).

In hindsight, Bobby Cremins' decision to offer John Salley a scholarship was a sure thing. At the time, though, Cremins was just looking for anybody who was tall and willing to come to Tech.

Salley wasn't highly recruited out of high school for a simple reason. "I was horrible," he said. Cremins agreed Salley wasn't very good. "I did not feel John was a bona fide college player," Cremins said, but he didn't really have much choice. "This was a rock-bottom program. The situation was so bad that if we could get anybody who was listed as six nine or six eight we were doing a good job."

So Salley came to Tech in 1982 an unknown and left in 1986 a star and one of the best players in the country. He established Tech's record for blocked shots and had his jersey retired. In 1991, he was inducted into the Georgia Tech Hall of Fame. He played twelve seasons in the NBA.

Along the way, John Salley obviously got a lot better. He had a strong desire to be a professional basketball player and went to work. "He made himself a player who would be a first-round draft pick," said sports psychologist Henry Kandel, who worked with the Tech team at the time. In addition to the Yellow Jacket team practices, Salley conducted solitary practice sessions. He found his motivation by remembering all the times he had been told he would never be a good ball player.

So he worked and he improved.

Even a Tech legend like John Salley had to work constantly to improve himself. So do you. You attend training sessions and seminars to do your job better. You take golf or tennis lessons and practice to get better. You play that new video game until you master it.

To get better at anything requires a regimen of practice, training, study, and preparation. This includes your faith. A Christian seeks not only to get to Heaven but also to live like Jesus on this Earth. Thus, to follow Jesus means you first of all must understand what Jesus taught about life and how to live. Then you put what you have learned into practice in your daily life, teaching others by example. You emulate Jesus by striving for the perfection he demonstrated in his life.

You get better as a Christian. You strive for perfection in your relationship with God, knowing that you will surely find it in eternity.

You have to listen to your assistant coaches. They're young and aggressive and always looking for a way to improve.

– Bobby Dodd

You work hard to get better in all phases of your life; that should include your faith.

DAY 59

DO WHAT YOU HAVE TO

Read 2 Samuel 12:1-15a.

"The Lord sent Nathan to David" (v. 1).

Bobby Dodd called it "the most depressing thing I ever had to do" – but he knew he had to do it.

"It" was the firing of two assistants and close friends in the wake of the 5-6 1950 season that had Dodd considering resigning. Adam Van Brimmer wrote, "Six seasons into what would become one of the greatest head coaching careers in college football history, Dodd's frustration with the talent level and inconsistent play of his Georgia Tech football team peaked."

Instead of resigning, though, in 1951 Dodd reluctantly made a series of moves that culminated with the change in assistants. For instance, he abhorred spring practice and often let his veteran players out of practice altogether, but not in 1951. Guard George Morris compared that spring to Bear Bryant's legendary first camp at Texas A&M, saying the difference was that Bryant "took his team to the desert" and Dodd took his to Rose Bowl Field. The practices that spring included full-contact scrimmages, another rite of football Dodd usually avoided.

Van Brimmer called that time in 1951 Dodd's "spring of desperation." The result, however, was a time that has been labeled the "Golden Era" of Georgia Tech football. As Dodd put it, "The sun came out." The Yellow Jackets would not lose again until the sixth week of the 1953 season, a thirty-one-game unbeaten streak.

The foundation for that success was laid when Bobby Dodd did some things he realized he had to even though in his heart he didn't want to.

You've also had to do some things you didn't want to. Maybe when you put your daughter on severe restriction, broke the news of a death in the family, fired a friend, or underwent surgery. You plowed ahead because you knew it was for the best or you had no choice.

Nathan surely didn't want to confront King David and tell him what a miserable reprobate he'd been, but the prophet had no choice: obedience to God overrode all other factors.

Of all that God asks of us in the living of a godly life, perhaps the most difficult is obedience. After all, our history of disobedience to God stretches all the way back to the Garden of Eden.

The problem is that God expects obedience not only when his wishes match our own but also when they don't. Obedience to God is a way of life, not a matter of convenience.

Coaching is making men do what they don't want, so they can become what they want to be.

-- Tom Landry

You can never foresee what God will demand of you, but obedience requires being ready to do whatever God asks.

DAY 60

MAKING UP

Read Matthew 5:21-24.

"If you are offering your gift at the altar and there remember that your brother has something against you, leave your gift there in front of the altar. First go and be reconciled to your brother" (vv. 23-24).

The Georgia Tech-Georgia baseball rivalry once got so heated that student bodies signed a peace treaty promising not to shoot opposing team members during a game or drop laxatives into their water buckets.

On May 9, 1919, the two schools were embroiled in a weekend series at Grant Field. Georgia led 2-1 in the bottom of the ninth, but Tech had a runner at second with only one out. That's when Tech's band members "arose from the stands and quickly trotted down to the first base line, instruments blaring, drums pounding" in an effort to rattle Georgia's pitcher. It didn't work. The Tech "stunt" and the Georgia win led to "general misbehavior by both sides" all afternoon and into the night. Georgia won the second game the next afternoon, and "boisterous behavior was the order of the day" again, including quite a few fist fights.

Officials from both schools arranged for a meeting between student representatives to draw up a peace treaty. *The Atlanta Constitution* said, "The old enemies joined hands and declared that in the future all the battling would be on the athletic field."

Among other matters, the students agreed not to use a shotgun on opposing team members during a game and not to poison opposing team members by putting laxatives in their water buckets. They also agreed that after each baseball game, the loser would retire gracefully, ceding the freedom of the city to the winners.

The student bodies further agreed unanimously "that the former German Kaiser should be hung."

College sports just wouldn't be as much fun if we didn't have rivalries with teams we love to insult, rail against, and whip the daylights out of. Our personal relationships are totally different, however, though sometimes a spirited disagreement with someone we love is worth it because the kissing and making up is so much fun. Making up carries an inherent problem, however, because for that reconciliation to occur, somebody must make the first move, which is always the hardest one. So often relationships in our lives are fractured simply because no one has the courage to be the first to attempt to make things right. We hide behind our wounded pride or injured feelings and allow a priceless relationship to wither and die.

The model in such a situation is Jesus. He not only told us to offer a hand and a hug, he lived it, surrendering his life so we could all get right with God.

Sport offers communities the opportunity to come together and reconcile; sport teaches important values such as respect, tolerance, solidarity, teamwork and fairness.

— Liberian official Adolf Ogi

Reconciliation takes courage; just ask Jesus, who died to get you right with God.

DAY 61

THE RIGHT PERSON

Read Matthew 26:47-50; 27:1-10.

"The betrayer had arranged a signal with them: 'The one I kiss is the man; arrest him.' Going at once to Jesus, Judas said, 'Greetings, Rabbi!' and kissed him" (vv. 48-49).

The powers that be were convinced Bobby Ross was the right man for the job.

Georgia Tech Athletic Director Homer Rice was on vacation in Florida on Jan. 3, 1987, when he learned his football coach, Bill Curry, had bolted for Alabama. Rice knew he needed to find a coach quickly, so his wife drove along I-75 while he jotted down the names of coaches from his days in the NFL and in college. "All of a sudden," Rice recalled, "I thought . . . Bobby Ross. Where is Bobby Ross?"

With a phone call made at the next I-75 exit, Rice learned Ross had taken a job as an assistant with the Buffalo Bills and was to start work in two days. Rice figured he had two things going for him: Ross would be a head coach, not an assistant, and he would be living in Atlanta, not Buffalo.

That evening Rice talked to Ross, and even though he hadn't talked to Tech's athletic board, Rice said, "If you're interested, . . . I'd like to go ahead and recommend you." After some more conversations, Rice persuaded Ross to fly to Atlanta and meet with the board without any guarantees even though to do so meant Ross gave up his job in Buffalo.

At the school president's home, Ross waited while Rice met with the board. The vote was unanimous; Ross was the new Tech head football coach. As the national championship of 1990 demonstrated, Bobby Ross was indeed the right man for the job.

What do you want to be when you grow up? Somehow you are supposed to know the answer to that question when you're a teenager, the time in life when common sense and logic are at their lowest ebb.

Long after those halcyon teen years are left behind, you may make frequent career changes. You chase the job that gives you not just financial rewards but also some personal satisfaction and sense of accomplishment. You desire a profession that uses your abilities, that you enjoy doing, and that gives you a sense of contributing to something bigger than yourself.

God, too, wants you in the right job, one that he has designed specifically for you. After all, even Judas was the right man for what God needed done. To do his work, God gave you abilities, talents, and passions. Do what you do best and what you love -- just do it for God.

A winner is someone who recognizes his God-given talents, works to develop them into skills, and uses these skills to accomplish his goals.
-- Larry Bird

God has a job for you, one for which he gave you particular talents, abilities, and passions.

CHOICES

Read Deuteronomy 30:15-20.

*"I have set before you life and death, blessings and curses.
Now choose life, so that you and your children may live"
(v. 19).*

Caitlin Lever had made her choice; now all she had to do was work up the nerve to tell her dad.

Lever grew up in Buffalo, N.Y., rifling hockey pucks. "Dad had me on skates from the beginning of time," she said. She was a center and right wing on two national-championship 19 & under club hockey teams while she was in high school. Hockey was in her genes; her dad is Don Lever, who played fifteen seasons in the NHL.

Lever never realized his dream of playing hockey for Canada in the Olympics, so he envisioned Caitlin in that role. Along the way, however, Caitlin realized that softball – not hockey -- was her first love. "It was ice hockey, ice hockey, and then getting the guts to admit to my dad it wasn't my love," she said.

When Caitlin told her dad, however, "He was more supportive than I expected." The senior Lever had no problem at all with softball; he wanted only that Caitlin get away from home to mature some. "Away from home" proved to be Atlanta and Georgia Tech. Her choice made, Caitlin set out to prove herself with a vengeance, and the result was excellence. "She's definitely the best every-day player I've ever had," Tech coach Sharon Perkins said.

In 2007, her senior season, she set a Tech season record for hits and on-base percentage. Three times All-ACC, she became only the second player in Tech history to garner first-team All-America honors.

And, oh, yes. In 2008, she played softball for Canada in the Summer Olympics.

As with Caitlin Lever, your life is the sum of the choices you've made. That is, you have arrived at this moment and this place in your life because of the choices you made in your past. Your love of the Yellow Jackets. Your spouse or the absence of one. Mechanic, teacher, or beautician. Condo in midtown Atlanta or ranch home in Warner Robins. Dog, cat, or goldfish. You chose; you live with the results.

That includes the most important choice you will ever have to make: faith or the lack of it. That we have the ability to make decisions when faced with alternatives is a gift from God, who allows that facility even when he's part of the choice. We can choose whether or not we will love him. God does remind us that this particular choice has rather extreme consequences: Choosing God's way is life; choosing against him is death.

Life or death. What choice is that?

The choices you make in life make you.

-- John Wooden

**God gives you the freedom to choose: life or death.
Is that really any choice at all?**

DAY 63

AT A LOSS

Read Philippians 3:7-11.

"I consider everything a loss compared to the surpassing greatness of knowing Christ Jesus my Lord, for whose sake I have lost all things" (v. 8).

Every time Jeremis Smith played a basketball game for Tech, he wore a reminder of what he had lost and what he had gained.

Smith finished his career on The Flats in 2008 as a three-year starter for Coach Paul Hewitt. He was the team captain both as a junior and a senior and wound up twelfth in career rebounds and eleventh in career steals.

On the night before he was to head to Atlanta from his home in Fort Worth in August 2005, he was sleeping when his mother woke him into a nightmare. A drunk driver on the wrong side of the highway had killed four teenagers, including Jeffrey Muriel, Jr., 19, one of Smith's closest friends. They called themselves "the J brothers" and had played basketball together since middle school.

"After [Jeffrey] died, it was real hard to concentrate in class," Smith recalled. He kept a drawing of the J brothers in his dorm room. "It seems like he's there, like he's talking back. . . . Sometimes I have moments when I have to be by myself and I cry my eyes out."

So Smith remembered, and as a reminder and a tribute, he wore four J's on his game shoes: 1) Jeremis himself, 2) a friend in Tech point guard Javaris Crittenton to remind him of what he had, 3) Jeffrey to remind him of what he had lost, and 4) Jesus to remind him of what Jeffrey and he had gained. "Two J's [are] looking down on the other two J's," Smith's mother said.

Maybe, as it was with Jeremis Smith, it was when a close friend died. Perhaps it wasn't so staggeringly tragic: your puppy died, your best friend moved away, or an older sibling left home. Sometime in your youth or early adult life, though, you learned that loss is a part of life.

Loss inevitably diminishes your life, but loss and the grief that accompanies it are part of the price of loving. When you first encountered loss, you learned that you were virtually helpless to prevent it or escape it.

There is life after loss, though, because you have one sure place to turn. As Jeremis knows, Jesus can share your pain and ease your suffering, but he doesn't stop there. Through the loss of his own life, he has transformed death -- the ultimate loss -- into the ultimate gain of eternal life. In Jesus lies the promise that one day loss itself will die.

To win, you have to risk loss.

-- Olympic champion skier Jean-Claude Killy

**Jesus not only eases the pain of our losses
but transforms the loss caused by death
into the gain of eternal life.**

DAY 64

BE PREPARED

Read Matthew 10:5-23.

"I am sending you out like sheep among wolves. Therefore be as shrewd as snakes and as innocent as doves" (v. 16).

His father kept telling him to get prepared, but Joe Burns didn't believe he would play football after high school.

From the time he was 5, Burns was a running back -- and he was good. Joe Burns, Sr. saw just how good his son was and exhorted him to get ready. "I had been telling him he needed to prepare himself," Dad said. "It never dawned on him what I was saying. He was satisfied playing in high school."

Son agreed with his father's assessment. "I never thought about going to college," Joe Jr. said. "I thought I'd graduate from high school and get a job." Many of those who cheered him in high school believed Burns just didn't have what it took to make it in college. Even the recruiters who loved his talent saw him as a significant academic risk because of his poor grades and his low SAT score.

But Burns' high school coach sat him down and got through to him. "He helped me get my priorities in order," Burns said. "I had to stop going places with my friends and concentrate on my books. It hit me I have a chance to play college football." Summer school, a Princeton Review course, two more tries at the SAT – and Burns was prepared for the academic rigors at Tech.

He led the Jackets in rushing in 1998 as a freshman, and in

2000 and 2001, the latter an All-ACC season. Burns turned pro after 2001, leaving The Flats as the fourth-leading rusher in Tech history.

You know the importance of preparation in your own life. You went to the bank for a car loan, facts and figures in hand. That presentation you made at work was seamless because you practiced. The kids' school play suffered no meltdowns because they rehearsed. Knowing what you need to do and doing what you must to succeed isn't luck; it's preparation.

Jesus understood this, and he prepared his followers by lecturing them and by sending them on field trips. Two thousand years later, the life of faith requires similar training and study. You prepare so you'll be ready when that unsaved neighbor standing beside you at your backyard grill asks about Jesus. You prepare so you will know how God wants you to live. You prepare so you are certain in what you believe when the secular, godless world challenges it.

And one day you'll see God face to face. You certainly want to be prepared for that.

Preparation is as necessary to successful coaching as weather is to the weather man; there must be some of it every day.

-- Bobby Dodd

Living in faith requires constant study and training, preparation for the day when you meet God face to face.

DAY 65

A SECOND CHANCE

Read John 7:53-8:11.

*"'Then neither do I condemn you,' Jesus declared.
'Go now and leave your life of sin'" (v. 8:11).*

Bobby Cremins got a second chance.

"Everybody thought I was crazy," he said of his decision in 1981 to leave Appalachian State for Georgia Tech, a foundering program in the country's toughest college basketball league. When Cremins arrived, Tech had gone 12-41 and 1-29 in league play in its first two years in the ACC. Some of what fans there were routinely showed up at games wearing paper bags over their heads.

So why did Cremins take the job? There were the obvious reasons. "The ACC was just a great conference. Tech was a great academic school. . . Atlanta is a big-time city. I thought the job had a lot of things to offer," he explained.

But there was another, perhaps more compelling reason that drove Cremins to Atlanta. He wanted a second chance; he wanted redemption.

He had played guard at South Carolina on the 1970 team heavily favored to win the ACC title and advance to the NCAA Tournament under Frank McGuire. But North Carolina State upset USC in overtime in the tournament finals after the ball was stolen from Cremins. Only one team from each league made it to the NCAA Tournament back then; South Carolina stayed at home.

"Not winning an ACC championship my senior year almost ruined by life," Cremins said. So Cremins came to Atlanta to win that ACC title he missed out on in 1970. He got it in 1985 (and 1990 and 1993). "That was the championship I lost," he said. "It took a lot of pain away for me."

"If I just had a second chance, I know I could make it work out." Ever said that? If only you could go back and tell your dad one last time you love him, take that job you passed up rather than relocate, or marry someone else. If only you had a second chance, a mulligan.

As the story of Jesus' encounter with the adulterous woman illustrates, with God you always get a second chance. No matter how many mistakes you make, God will never give up on you. Nothing you can do puts you beyond God's saving power. You always have a second chance because with God your future is not determined by your past or who you used to be. It is determined by your relationship with God through Jesus Christ.

God is ready and willing to give you a second chance – or a third chance or a fourth chance – if you will give him a chance.

I have to thank God for giving me the gift that he did as well as a second chance for a better life.
-- Olympics figure skating champion Oksana Baiul

You get a second chance with God
if you give him a chance.

DAY 66

IN GOD'S OWN TIME

Read Colossians 3:12-17.

"Therefore, as God's chosen people, holy and dearly loved, clothe yourselves with compassion, kindness, humility, gentleness and patience" (v. 12).

Tech could only wait – and hope.

With a 45-21 blistering of Nebraska in the 1991 Citrus Bowl, the Yellow Jackets finished their season 11-0-1, the nation's only undefeated team. But would they be national champions? They went into the game ranked behind a Colorado team that had a loss and a tie. "I felt we deserved it," Coach Bobby Ross said of the title.

But Colorado edged Notre Dame in the Orange Bowl, and basketball coach Bobby Cremins expressed the sentiment of many of the Tech faithful when he said, "That was our national championship right there." As Jack Wilkinson put it, "Colorado had precedent and prejudice on its side. No No. 1 team that won a bowl game had ever been bumped from the top spot." Moreover, the sports writers that voted in the AP poll considered the ACC a basketball conference and thus questioned Tech's schedule and credentials.

Tech's wait stretched until the afternoon of Jan. 2 and ended with confirmation of the Jackets' fears: The AP voted Colorado the national champions; Tech was No. 2.

The votes of the coaches in the UPI poll were still coming in, though, so the tense waiting went on with hopes of a split championship. About four o'clock that afternoon, Tech officials learned the Jackets were in the lead but all ballots weren't in. The nail-biting wait continued until a phone call revealed the Jackets were UPI champs by one vote. "Justice was done," quarterback Shawn Jones said.

The wait had ended; the celebration had begun.

Have you ever left a restaurant because the server didn't take your order quickly enough? Complained at your doctor's office about how long you had to wait? Wondered how much longer a sermon was going to last?

It isn't just the machinations of the world with which we're impatient; we want God to move at our pace, not his. For instance, how often have you prayed and expected – indeed, demanded – an immediate answer from God? And aren't Christians the world over impatient for the glorious day when Jesus will return and set everything right? We're in a hurry but God obviously isn't.

As rare as it seems to be, patience is nevertheless included among the likes of gentleness, humility, kindness, and compassion as attributes of a Christian.

God expects us to be patient. He knows what he's doing, he is in control, and his will shall be done. On his schedule, not ours.

I was born and raised on a farm, and when you watch those crops grow, you learn to be patient.

-- Pat Dye

God moves in his own time, so often we must wait for him to act, remaining faithful and patient.

TEN TO REMEMBER

Read Exodus 20:1-17.

"God spoke all these words: 'I am the Lord your God . . . .
You shall have no other gods before me'" (vv. 1, 3).

With more than 650 wins in its football history, Georgia Tech has had quite a few runaways over the years with the biggest coming in the early days.

Any list of Tech's lopsided wins always begins with the 222-0 win over Cumberland in 1916. Tech scored 32 touchdowns and had 978 yards of offense without ever throwing a pass. Neither team made a first down in the game as Cumberland couldn't and Tech scored within four downs on every possession. Since Cumberland lost yardage on every play, the Tennessee boys eventually adopted the unique strategy of punting the ball back to Tech on the first play after a Tech kickoff.

But Tech has broken the century mark on four other occasions, all during the John Heisman years. The 1918 team went 6-1, averaging more than 77 points a game in its wins. Three times the team scored more than 100 points: 128-0 over N.C. State, 123-0 over the 11th Cavalry, 118-0 over Furman. The 1914 Golden Tornado buried Mercer 105-0. The 1917 national champions almost added another triple-digit win to Tech history, rolling over Carlisle 98-0.

Rounding out the top ten all-time margins of victory are an 83-0 romp over Vanderbilt in 1917, a 77-0 slaughter of Florida in 1904 (Heisman's first season at Tech), a 74-0 win over Furman in 1919, and a pair of 70-0 romps, over Dahlonega in 1907 and Davidson in 1921. William Alexander coached that last win.

These are indeed ten margins of victory for Tech fans to remember.

You've got your list and you're ready to go: a gallon of paint and a water hose from the hardware store; chips, peanuts, and sodas from the grocery store for tonight's card game with your buddies; the tickets for the band concert. Your list helps you remember.

God made a list once of things he wanted you to remember: the Ten Commandments. Just as your list reminds you to do something, so does God's list remind you of how you are to act in your dealings with other people and with him.

A life dedicated to Jesus is a life devoted to relationships, and God's list emphasizes that the social life and the spiritual life of the faithful cannot be sundered. God's relationship to you is one of unceasing, unqualified love, and you are to mirror that divine love in your relationships with others. In case you forget, you have a list.

Society today treats the Ten Commandments as if they were the ten suggestions. Never compromise on right or wrong.
-- *College baseball coach Gordie Gillespie*

God's list is a set of instructions on how you are to conduct yourself with other people and with him.

DAY 68

ANSWERING THE CALL

Read 1 Samuel 3:1-18.

"The Lord came and stood there, calling as at the other times, 'Samuel! Samuel!' Then Samuel said, 'Speak, for your servant is listening'" (v. 10).

Gerris Wilkinson certainly didn't want to do it – he had no say in the whole matter -- but he switched to defensive end for the good of the team.

Wilkinson clearly preferred to line up at outside linebacker, which he had played as a Yellow Jacket freshman in 2002. In fact, he had never played from a down stance, so as the 2003 season neared, he expected to be a factor in the Tech linebacking corps.

But the Tech defensive line took several hits from injuries and grades; Chan Gailey and his coaches had to plug the holes as best they could – and Wilkinson was one of the best. They told him right before the start of fall camp that the team needed him at defensive end. Wilkinson made the move without comment or complaint.

Undersized at 6-foot-3, 230 pounds, Wilkinson made up for it with his quickness and overall athleticism. He started every game in 2003 with twelve tackles for loss, four sacks, two pass break-ups, a fumble recovery, and 42 tackles as the Jackets went to the Humanitarian Bowl and buried Tulsa 52-10. "I did better than I expected myself to do," Wilkinson admitted.

Gailey agreed and praised Wilkinson's willingness to make

the move. The former NFL coach pointed out that Wilkinson's proven versatility would enhance his stock with the pros, which was borne out when he was drafted in the third round in 2006 by the New York Giants. Back as a linebacker in 2004 and 2005, Wilkinson was twice All-ACC.

Gerris Wilkinson answered the call.

A team player is someone who does whatever the coach calls upon him to do for the good of the team. Something quite similar occurs when God places a specific call upon a Christian's life.

This is much scarier, though, than shifting positions on a football team as Gerris Wilkinson did. The way many folks understand it is that answering God's call means going into the ministry, packing the family up, and moving halfway around the world to some place where folks have never heard of air conditioning, fried chicken, paved roads, or the Georgia Tech Yellow Jackets. Zambia. The Philippines. Cleveland even.

Not for you, no thank you. And who can blame you?

But God usually calls folks to serve him where they are. In fact, God put you where you are right now, and he has a purpose in placing you there. Wherever you are, are you serving him?

It was like being in a foreign country.
-- Welsh soccer player Ian Rush on playing in Italy

**Serving God doesn't necessarily mean entering
full-time ministry and going to a foreign land;
God calls you to serve him where you are now.**

DAY 69

UNDERDOG

Read 1 Samuel 17:17-50.

"David said to the Philistine, . . . 'This day the Lord will hand you over to me, and I'll strike you down'" (vv. 45-46).

Tech's great run to the Final Four in 1990 included a second-round game that remains one of the greatest in school history.

On March 17, the opponent was LSU, and the game was the basketball equivalent of David vs. Goliath, the giant being LSU's twin towers of 7-foot-1 Shaquille O'Neal and 7-footer Stanley Roberts. Even the Jackets were impressed. During the warmups, Johnny McNeil, who would give up three inches and 70 pounds to O'Neal, turned to Malcolm Mackey, no runt at 6-10, and exclaimed, "Will you look at these guys?"

And when the game started, Tech's worst nightmares came true. "I don't know if they intimidated my team, but they intimidated me," Coach Bobby Cremins said. Over the first ten minutes, LSU seemed to block every shot the Jackets put up. "I thought for a while we weren't going to get a shot off," assistant coach Sherman Dillard said.

LSU led 22-5 before Cremins' move to a small lineup with three guards began to pay off. When Kenny Anderson nailed a shot with nine seconds left, Tech trailed only 41-40 at halftime.

The Jackets led eight different times in the second half until Anderson drove the lane with 1:35 left to give Tech the lead for good at 92-91. Though LSU controlled the ball for 93 of the last 95 seconds, Tech's relentless defense kept the Tigers at bay for the 94-91 win.

Perhaps the most incredible statistic of the game was that Tech outrebounded LSU 52-51. On this day, David had once again nailed Goliath.

You probably don't gird your loins, pick up a slingshot and some smooth, round river rocks, and go out to battle ill-tempered giants regularly. You do, however, fight each day to make some economic and social progress and to keep the ones you love safe, sheltered, and protected. Armed only with your pluck, your knowledge, your wits, and your hustle, in many ways you are an underdog; the best you can hope for is that the world is indifferent. You need all the weapons you can get.

How about using the ultimate weapon David had: the absolute, unshakable conviction that when he tackled opposition of any size, he would prevail. He knew this because he did everything for God's glory and therefore God was in his corner. If you imitate David's lifestyle by glorifying God in everything you do, then God is there for you when you need him. Who's the underdog then?

Always remember that Goliath was a 40-point favorite over Little David.

-- Shug Jordan

**Living to glorify God is the lifestyle
of a champion.**

DAY 70

THE SCAPEGOAT

Read Leviticus 16:15-22.

"He is to lay both hands on the head of the live goat and confess over it all the wickedness and rebellion of the Israelites — all their sins — and put them on the goat's head" (v. 21).

Roy Riegels "was sport's original goat."

Riegels is so irreparably tied up with the history of Georgia Tech football that he is a member of the lettermen's club though he played for an opponent. Riegels earned one of college football's most enduring monikers – "Wrong Way" -- against Tech in the 1929 Rose Bowl. A linebacker for the California Bears, he caught a Tech fumble and returned it the wrong way in one of college football's most famous plays.

When halfback Jack "Stumpy" Thomason fumbled at the Tech 35, Riegels picked the ball out of midair and turned to run. Riegels would later say, "I completely lost my bearings." A Cal halfback tried to turn him around, but Riegels thought the player wanted the ball and kept running. Finally, the Cal player grabbed Riegels and turned him around short of the goal line where Tech players tackled him.

Officials spotted the ball at the one, and Cal elected to punt on first down. Tech's Vance Maree blocked the kick for a safety and Tech led 2-0.

At halftime, Riegels was inconsolable, telling his coach he'd ruined the game and that he couldn't face the crowd. The coach convinced him otherwise, and Riegels, who would be All-America the following season, made several tackles and blocked a Tech punt in the second half.

But as fate would have it, Tech scored and Cal responded late with a touchdown. The final score was 8-7; the safety was the difference. "Wrong Way" Roy Riegels was the Rose Bowl goat.

A particular type of goat -- a scapegoat – could really be useful. Mess up at work? Bring him in to get chewed out. Make a decision your children don't like? Let her put up with the whining and complaining. Forget your anniversary? Call him in to grovel and explain.

What a set-up! You don't have to pay the price for your mistakes, your shortcomings, and your failures. You get off scot-free. Exactly the way forgiveness works with Jesus.

Our sins separate us from God because we the unholy can't stand in the presence of the holy God. To remove our guilt, God requires a blood sacrifice. Out of his unimaginable love for us, he provided the sacrifice – his own son. Jesus is the sacrifice made for us; through Jesus and Jesus alone, forgiveness and eternity with God are ours. It's a bumper sticker, but it's true: We aren't perfect; we're just forgiven.

I never blame myself when I'm not hitting. I just blame the bat, and if it keeps up, I change bats.

– *Yogi Berra*

**For all those times you fail God, you have Jesus
to take the guilt and the blame for you.**

DAY 71

FLAT BUSTED

Read Luke 16:1-15.

"You cannot serve both God and money" (v. 13b).

Bill Curry faced a number of problems when he took over as head coach of the Tech football team in 1980 – not the least of which was that the program was flat broke.

Curry played as a center and a linebacker at Tech under Bobby Dodd, graduating in 1964. In the search for a successor to Pepper Rodgers, Tech's athletic board "thought it was important to bring in someone who could understand not only the importance of Tech's athletic tradition, but who could unite the alumni." That someone was Bill Curry, who was the unanimous choice of the board despite his having no head coaching experience. "Bill Curry was such a natural fit for Georgia Tech," said Jacket basketball coach Bobby Cremins.

But times were not good on The Flats. As Kim King put it, "It would be a rocky road until [Curry] got his program established." Tech's campus newspaper wrote, "Football attendance was down, basketball excitement was low and baseball was just as bad." Curry found a much bigger problem than indifference; Tech's athletic program was broke. "We were bankrupt in every way," Curry recalled. He teamed with a few others and "literally begged the students to increase the athletic fee $15 per quarter just to pay the bills."

But the turnaround had begun all across campus with Curry, Cremins, and baseball coach Jim Morris. The Jackets went 6-4-1 in 1984 and 9-2-1 in 1985, beating Georgia both years. Tech people came back to the games, bringing with them money for the athletic coffers.

Having a little too much money at the end of the month may be as bothersome -- if not as worrisome -- as having a little too much month at the end of the money. The investment possibilities are bewildering: stocks, bonds, mutual funds, that group pooling their money to open up a neighborhood coffee shop -- that's a good idea.

You take your money seriously, as well you should. Jesus, too, took money seriously, warning us frequently of its dangers. Money itself is not evil; its peril lies in the ease with which it can usurp God's rightful place as the master of our lives.

Certainly in our age and society, we often measure people by how much money they have. But like our other talents, gifts, and resources, money should primarily be used for God's purposes. God's love must touch not only our hearts but our wallets also.

How much of your wealth are you investing with God?

Money can buy you everything but happiness. It can pay your fare to everywhere but heaven.

-- Pete Maravich

Your attitude about money says much about your attitude toward God.

THE ANSWER

Read Colossians 2:2-10.

*"My purpose is that they . . . may know the mystery of
God, namely, Christ, in whom are hidden all the treasures
of wisdom and knowledge" (vv. 2, 3).*

Accosted by legendary Kentucky basketball coach Adolph
Rupp, Whack Hyder had an answer for him. Twice in fact.

Once described as "the quintessential goodwill ambassador
for Georgia Tech," Hyder was a Tech man from start to finish.
Reviewing his life, he said, "Thirty-eight years I was on the
Tech campus as a student, a teacher in the P.E. Department and
as a coach. It's my whole life, really." For 22 years, Hyder was
the Tech basketball coach. When he stepped down in 1973, he
was the winningest coach in school history with 292 victories, a
mark broken by Bobby Cremins, who won 354 games.

Hyder joined the Tech staff in 1946 as the freshman coach. Five
years later, he stopped by Athletic Director Bobby Dodd's office
to discuss the head coaching job. His interview consisted of seven
words from Dodd: "Hello, Whack, You're our new basketball
coach." It seems some of the varsity players had asked Dodd to
hire Hyder.

Once before a game against SEC rival and kingpin Kentucky,
the acerbic Rupp asked Hyder how he intended to win in the old
gym he had. Hyder responded that he wanted three things from
his players: "I want them to live a good, Christian life. Next I want

them to study and get a good education. And third, I want them to give me their time in basketball." Rupp scoffed at that reply.

But Hyder wasn't through giving the coach answers. The next night his Yellow Jackets upset Rupp's top-ranked Wildcats – for the second time that season.

Experience is essentially the uncovering of answers to some of life's questions, both trivial and profound. You often discover to your dismay that as soon as you learn a few answers, the questions change. Your children get older, your health worsens, your financial situation changes, one of Tech's teams struggles unexpectedly -- all situations requiring answers to a new set of difficulties.

No answers, though, are more important than those you seek in your search for God and the meaning of life because they determine your fate for all eternity. Since a life of faith is a journey and not a destination, the questions do indeed change with your circumstances. The "why" or the "what" you ask God when you're a teenager is vastly different from the quandaries you ponder as an adult. No matter how you phrase the question, though, the answer inevitably centers on Jesus. And that answer never changes.

When you're a driver and you're struggling in the car, you're looking for God to come out of the sky and give you a magical answer.
-- NASCAR's Rusty Wallace

It doesn't matter what the question is;
if it has to do with life, temporal or eternal,
the answer lies in Jesus.

DAY 73

MIDDLE OF NOWHERE

Read Genesis 28:10-22.

"When Jacob awoke from his sleep, he thought, 'Surely the Lord is in this place, and I was not aware of it'" (v. 16).

On the strength of a tractor and a horse, Durant Brooks came to Tech from the middle of nowhere – "one crossing light, a grocery store, and maybe two gas stations" was the way Brooks described it – and he left The Flats as the best punter in the nation.

Brooks' home is Gordon, Ga., about thirty miles east of Macon. "Blink, and you'll miss it," he said.

The tractor came into play when he was in his grandmother's front yard where he'd "start punting. . . . Sometimes, I'd get out in a field, but I'd have to get the tractor out and cut me a lane."

And the horse? Brooks grew up fox hunting with the full regalia including English saddles, which have no horn to grab. Brooks vows that's how he developed such a strong leg because "more or less, you have to hold on with your legs."

And he did develop quite a leg. In his two years at Tech (2006-07), he punted 144 times; an incredible 57 of them were longer than 50 yards. He left The Flats averaging 45.31 yards per punt, the best in Tech history. In the 2007 game against North Carolina (which Tech won 27-25), he set a school record by averaging 60 yards per punt.

Brooks was first-team All-ACC and second-team All-America both years. His senior year he became the first punter in Tech history to win the Ray Guy Award, awarded to the nation's best collegiate punter.

A tractor and a horse helped Durant Brooks leave the middle of nowhere.

Ever been to Gordon? Or Meigs? How about Ty Ty or Odum, which is just down the road from Surrency? And don't miss Tignall if you're on the way to Norman.

They are among the many small communities that dot the Georgia countryside. Off the interstates and often more than a few miles from a good-sized town, they seem to be in the middle of nowhere, the type of place where Durant Brooks mowed with a tractor and went fox hunting. They're hamlets we just zip through on our way to somewhere really important.

But don't be misled; those villages are indeed special and wonderful. That's because God is in Mineral Bluff and Subligna just as he is in downtown Atlanta, Columbus, and Savannah. Even when you are far off the roads well traveled, you are with God. The middle of nowhere is, in fact, holy ground -- because God is there.

The middle of nowhere is the place that teaches you that crossing the goal line first is not as important as the course you took to get there.
— Dive instructor Ridlon Kiphart

**No matter how far off the beaten path you travel,
you are still on holy ground because God is there.**

THE FAME GAME

Read 1 Kings 10:1-10, 18-29.

"King Solomon was greater in riches and wisdom than all the other kings of the earth. The whole world sought audience with Solomon" (vv. 23-24).

Robert Tyre Jones II is still Tech's most famous athlete. Bobby Jones graduated from the Institute in 1920 with a degree in mechanical engineering. He played for the school's golf team, and one dean remembered him as "a real gentleman in every respect, modest, unassuming, never mentioning his golf fame."

Jones' enduring fame comes not from his days at Tech but from his reputation as "the greatest amateur golfer ever." From 1923 to 1930, he won thirteen major championships and 62 percent of the events he entered. On Sept. 27, 1930, he "walked off the 11th green at the Merion Cricket Club [in Ardmore, Penn.] and into history," accomplishing a feat unequaled before or since. He won the Grand Slam, all four of golf's major championships – the U.S. and British opens and the U.S. and British amateur championships – in a single season.

Former PGA Tour Commissioner Joe Dey credited Jones with creating today's Grand Slam. "When Jones retired, there was not another amateur of his ability, and after he started Augusta National [and the Masters], . . . attention turned away from the amateurs to the professionals," Dey said. "What Jones did was win the Grand Slam, then without realizing it, created another one."

From the time he was 14 until he retired from competitive golf at 28, no player ever beat him twice in championship play. In the last eleven British and U.S. opens he played, he won seven and finished no worse than second ten times.

A legendary hero, Bobby Jones remains famous long after his death in 1971.

Have you ever wanted to be famous? Hanging out with other rich and famous people, having people listen to what you say, throwing money around like toilet paper, meeting adoring and clamoring fans, signing autographs, and posing for the paparazzi before you climb into your imported sports car?

Many of us yearn to be famous, well-known in the places and by the people that we believe matter. That's all fame amounts to: strangers knowing your name and your face.

The truth is that you are already famous where it really does matter, which excludes TV's talking heads, screaming teenagers, moviegoers, or D.C. power brokers. You are famous because God knows your name, your face, and everything about you.

If a persistent photographer snapped you pondering this fame – the only kind that has eternal significance – would the picture show the world unbridled joy or the shell-shocked expression of a mug shot?

When you play a sport, you have two things in mind. One is to get into the Hall of Fame and the other is to go to heaven when you die.
– Lee Trevino

You're already famous because God knows
your name and your face, which may be either
reassuring or terrifying.

DAY 75

THE GOOD OLD DAYS

Read Psalm 102.

"My days vanish like smoke; . . . but you remain the same, and your years will never end" (vv. 3, 27).

Ever long for the "good old days" of college football, what you probably consider a simpler time? Well, just consider the first-ever football game between Tech and Georgia – and maybe those old days don't seem so good after all.

The two first played each on Saturday, Nov. 4, 1893, in Athens. The great rivalry began at 3:15 on a field 110 yards long with two 30-minute halves. With no forward passes, strategy consisted of pounding away on the ground. Playing for Tech, Lt. Leonard Wood, surgeon general at Fort McPherson, scored the series' first touchdown to get Tech off and running to an 18-0 halftime lead.

Another score early in the last half upped the lead to 22-0, and the folks from Athens weren't taking too kindly to the beating they were receiving. *The Atlanta Journal* reported that "a stone was hurled at one of the Tech players, striking him a cruel blow in the head while he was on the ground." The missile didn't necessarily come from a player since the crowd had the run of the field with the players. The *Journal* reported another instance in which one "Athenian" pulled a knife and threatened a Tech player. "The Techs were also poked and gouged with canes on plays toward the boundary lines."

Tech eventually won 28-6. To cap the day off, the train carrying the players home ran into a stalled freight train. Since the freight was headed for Atlanta, the uninjured players simply "hopped aboard and chugged on," arriving home after midnight.

Maybe today's game and atmosphere are quite a bit better than the "good old days" of 1893.

It's a brutal truth that time just never stands still. The current of your life sweeps you along until you realize one day you've lived long enough to have a past. Part of it you cling to fondly. The stunts you pulled with your high-school buddies. Your first apartment. That dance with your first love. That special vacation. Those "good old days."

You hold on relentlessly to the memory of those old, familiar ways because of the stability they provide in our uncertain world. They will always be there even as times change and you age.

Another constant exists in your life too. God has been a part of every event in your life that created a memory because he was there. He's always there with you; the question is whether you ignore him or make him a part of your day.

A "good old day" is any day shared with God.

Years ago, you used to get out and fight and run around and chase each other with a jackhammer and stuff like that. Those were the good old days.

> -- *Dale Earnhardt Jr., on NASCAR track etiquette*

**Today is one of the "good old days" if you share it
with God.**

IN THE KNOW

Read John 4:19-26, 39-42.

"They said to the woman, . . . 'Now we have heard for ourselves, and we know that this man really is the Savior of the world'" (v. 42).

That doggone Dodd Luck, you can't beat it." *Dodd's Luck* was even the title of Bobby Dodd's biography. In reality, though, Dodd's coaching success had little to do with luck. Bear Bryant knew; "Dodd's luck was really Dodd smart," he said.

Not to say that Dodd didn't use the reputation of his luck to his advantage. "Think you're lucky and you will be," he said, knowing that if his opponents believed in Dodd's luck, they were at a mental disadvantage, for they would play as if they were waiting for something to happen.

Dodd's luck – and the reality behind it – was never illustrated any better than the 1965 Gator Bowl. The 6-3-1 Yellow Jackets were matched against 10th-ranked Texas Tech. The favored Red Raiders were led by a great back named Donnie Anderson. They also featured a tough defense.

Kim King, the Jacket quarterback said, "During practice all week, nobody thought that we'd be able to run against Texas Tech, that we would have to throw every down." The Jackets certainly wanted to keep the ball away from Anderson.

So Dodd called his team together right before kickoff and announced, "Men, if we win the coin toss, we'll kick." King joined his teammates in their reaction: "What?" And then Dodd explained: "I watched them in warmups. They're tight."

On Texas Tech's first series – after the Jackets won the toss and kicked off – Anderson fumbled. Georgia Tech scored, Texas Tech never recovered, and the Jackets won easily 31-21.

No luck to it. Bobby Dodd just knew.

He knew about Texas Tech in the same way you know certain things in your life. That your spouse loves you, for instance. That you are good at your job. That tea should be iced and sweetened. That a bad day fishing is still better than a good day at work. That the best barbecue comes from a pig. You know these things even though no mathematician or philosopher can prove any of this on paper.

It's the same way with faith in Jesus: You just know that he is God's son and the savior of the world. You know it in the same way that you know Georgia Tech is the only team worth pulling for: with every fiber of your being, with all your heart, your mind, and your soul.

You just know, and because you know him, Jesus knows you. And that is all you really need to know.

It's what you learn after you think you know it all that counts.
-- Earl Weaver

A life of faith is lived in certainty and conviction:
You just know you know.

CONFIDENCE MAN

Read Micah 7:5-7.

"As for me, I will look to the Lord, I will wait for the God of my salvation" (v. 7 NRSV).

On the bus ride to the 1989 Clemson game, offensive tackle Darryl Jenkins looked over to Kevin Bryant, Tech's director of marketing and promotions, and declared, "You know, we're going to kick Clemson."

Many Tech fans would have thought Jenkins' confidence misplaced; the Clemson faithful would have scoffed and said it was downright ludicrous. The 14th-ranked Tigers were a 20-point favorite, holding Tech in such low regard that the Jackets were the homecoming hors d'oeuvre. Still, Bryant said, Jenkins felt it wasn't even going to be a close game – and Jenkins wasn't alone. The Jackets arrived in Clemson that Oct. 14 brimming with a confidence surprising for a 1-3 team.

The confidence was a carryover from the week before when Tech had fallen behind the Maryland Terrapins 14-0 in the second quarter. In what was to become one of the most pivotal games in Tech's eventual ascension to the national title in 1990, quarterback Shawn Jones and his teammates "suddenly became fireproof, and foolproof." "A lot of guys got ticked off, like, 'This is ending right here,'" Jones said.

With Maryland leading 21-7 in the third quarter, Jones threw three touchdown passes in just over ten minutes: a 9-yarder to

Tom Covington, a 5-yarder to fullback Stefen Scotton that tied the game, and a 26-yarder to Covington for a 28-21 lead. Maryland managed only a field goal in the fourth quarter, and Tech had a 28-24 win.

And how did the newfound confidence play out against Clemson? As Jenkins had predicted, the game wasn't close; Tech rolled 30-14.

You need confidence in all areas of your life. You're confident the company you work for will pay you on time, or you wouldn't go to work. You turn the ignition confident your car will start. When you flip a switch, you expect the light to come on.

Confidence in other people and in things is often misplaced, though. Companies go broke; car batteries die; light bulbs burn out. Even the people you love the most sometimes let you down.

So where can you place your trust with absolute confidence you won't be betrayed? In the promises of God.

Such confidence is easy, of course, when everything's going your way, but what about when you cry as Micah did, "What misery is mine!" As Micah declares, that's when your confidence in God must be its strongest. That's when you wait for the Lord confident that God will not fail you, that he will never let you down.

When it gets right down to the wood-chopping, the key to winning is confidence.

-- Darrell Royal

People, things, and organizations will let you down; only God can be trusted absolutely and confidently.

DAY 78

FINDERS KEEPERS

Read Luke 11:5-13.

"So I say to you: Ask and it will be given to you; seek and you will find" (v. 9).

As a game with the Clemson Tigers neared in January 1936, the Georgia Tech basketball players didn't have the game on their minds. Instead, they were prowling around looking for bugs.

Most of the players were enrolled in a biology class and had to assemble a collection of bugs as an assignment prior to finals. Bill Ballew wrote, the players "scoured all the normal places – under logs and stones and in and around trees and bushes." Some of the players bought shovels and turned earth at various locations around campus. A recent cold snap, however, rendered their dig fruitless – and bugless.

The desperate players even turned to Athletic Director William Alexander for help. "I know where you can find some very fine worms," Alexander told them. Worms wouldn't help, though termites would do the trick, the players replied. Alexander then suggested they scour some of Atlanta's older hotels to find some of the wood-chomping insects.

The players evidently didn't follow that advice, for the search continued with *The Atlanta Constitution* stepping in to help. Said the paper, "If anyone knows where there is to be found a nice batch of bugs, Tech basketball players would appreciate getting the information."

The evasive and elusive bugs were located and assembled in time for finals, allowing the players to turn their attention to Clemson. They had more success finding the bugs than they did finding the basket, however, as the Tigers defeated the Jackets 39-31 on Jan. 25, 1936.

While we may not be scouring dark, wet places for beetles and stinkbugs, we are all continuously looking for something in our lives. It may be love, a satisfying career, peace of mind, good health, a church where we feel welcome, a nice home and neighborhood in which to live, but it's always something. We are basically needy people, though the exact nature of the needs may vary during our lives.

God knows this; after all, he put the hunger into our souls. So Jesus came along and offered a practical solution: He told us to pray. In fact, Jesus admonished us to be bold, confident, and persistent in our prayers. In the ongoing process of prayer, we come to a realization of our total, complete dependence upon God. We further come to understand God's loving and giving character.

God is open to our prayers, but we must seek him out in faith, not just in need.

I've always asked for good health, wisdom, and help me to try to be good. I definitely believe in prayer.

— Bobby Bowden

Bringing our need to God's love in faith is called prayer.

DAY 79

NAME DROPPING

Read Exodus 3:1-15.

"This is my name forever, the name by which I am to be remembered from generation to generation" (v. 15).

Chappell Rhino will probably forever be remembered by the Tech faithful as "One-Play" Rhino.

The father of Tech All-America Randy Rhino (1971-74), Chappell Rhino was a star on the Yellow Jacket baseball team. On the football team, though, he was a seldom used defensive back. He made his mark and acquired his nickname as a senior in 1952.

Tech went into the Georgia game with a 24-game unbeaten streak. A win over the 6-3 Bulldogs would give the Jackets a second consecutive unbeaten season and a shot at the national championship. An early fumble set up a Georgia touchdown before a Pepper Rodgers field goal made it 7-3 at halftime.

In the third quarter, Tech drove to a fourth and four at the Georgia ten. Coach Bobby Dodd decided to go for it, calling for a running pass, a staple of the Jacket offense. But acting on a hunch that was yet another instance of the peculiarly Dodd genius, he inserted Rhino into the game to throw the pass. Offensive coordinator Frank Broyles said he couldn't recall Rhino ever throwing a pass in practice. But Dodd insisted. "I thought Chappell was enough of an athlete to where he could do it for me," Dodd later said.

Dodd was right. Rhino took the toss from quarterback Bill

Brigman, ran to his right, and hit receiver Buck Martin for a touchdown. It was Rhino's only play of the game, but it propelled the Jackets to a 23-9 win and the undefeated season and gave rise to Rhino's unique nickname.

Nicknames such as "One-Play" Rhino are not slapped haphazardly upon individuals but rather reflect widely held perceptions about the person named. Proper names do that also.

Nowhere throughout history has this concept been more prevalent that in the Bible, where a name is not a mere label but is an expression of the essential nature of the named one. That is, a person's name reveals his or her character. Even God shares this concept; to know the name of God is to know God as he has chosen to reveal himself to us.

What does your name say about you? Honest, trustworthy, a seeker of the truth and a person of God? Or does the mention of your name cause your coworkers to whisper snide remarks, your neighbors to roll their eyes, or your friends to stammer as they try to make allowances for you?

Most importantly, what does your name say about you to God? He, too, knows you by name.

The Yellow Jacket nickname did not grow out of the six-legged insect, but rather was first used to describe Tech supporters who attended events dressed in yellow coats and jackets.
--- 2008 Georgia Tech football media guide

Live so that your name evokes positive associations by people you know, the public, and God.

DAY 80

AS YOU SEE IT

Read John 20:11-18.

"Mary stood outside the tomb crying" (v. 11).

For Kim King, a meeting between Bobby Dodd and three rich friends of his to kick off a massive fund-raising campaign was a bust, but, boy, did he have it all wrong.

In the mid 1970s, the effort began to raise millions of dollars to modernize Georgia Tech's athletic facilities. The result would be the $7-million Arthur B. Edge Intercollegiate Athletics Center, dedicated in 1982.

That day was years away, though, when King, the former Tech quarterback whom Tech president Joe Pettit had made chairman of the fund-raising, Coach Dodd, and athletic director Doug Weaver flew to Houston for the first solicitation of funds. King's high hopes were dampened when one of their targets met them at the airport. He wore an old white shirt and a stained string tie and drove an old clunker that threatened to wheeze mightily and die at any moment. King thought, "Who is this gardener they sent to pick us up?"

After the six men ate lunch and told tall tales about old times, Dodd made his pitch. To King's dismay, one man said, "Bobby, I'll give you five hundred." The second added five hundred, the third two-fifty. King's total: $1,250.

For the only time in his life, King was angry at Dodd. He

pointed out that the plane tickets alone to Houston had cost $1,600. Dodd patiently laid a hand on his former player and said, "Oh, no, Kimmy. They're talking about a million and two hundred and fifty thousand dollars."

An embarrassed King had had the wrong perspective on the whole meeting.

Your perspective goes a long way toward determining whether you slink through life amid despair, anger, and hopelessness or stride boldly through life with joy and hope. Mary is a good example. On that first Easter morning, she stood by Jesus' tomb crying, her heart broken, because she still viewed everything through the perspective of Jesus' death. But how her attitude, her heart, and her life changed when she saw the morning through the perspective of Jesus' resurrection.

So it is with life and death for all of us. You can't avoid death, but you can determine how you perceive it. Is it fearful, dark, fraught with peril and uncertainty? Or is it a simple little passageway to glory, the light, and loved ones, an elevator ride to paradise?

It's a matter of perspective that depends totally on whether or not you're standing by Jesus' side when it arrives.

For some people it's the end of the rainbow, but for us it's the end of the finish line.

– Rower Larisa Healy

Whether death is your worst enemy or a solicitous chauffeur is a matter of perspective.

DAY 81

ANGER MANAGEMENT

Read James 1:19-27.

"Everyone should be quick to listen, slow to speak and slow to become angry, for man's anger does not bring about the righteous life that God desires" (vv. 19-20).

Craig Page was mad with Georgia Tech. It's a good thing he didn't stay that way.

Page is one of the greatest offensive linemen in Jacket history. He capped his career on The Flats with a sensational senior season in 1998. He won the Jacobs Award, presented to the ACC's top blocker. He was first-team All-ACC and first-team All-America. He was a finalist for the Outland Trophy, won by the nation's best interior lineman, and went on to a career in the NFL.

He didn't start his college career in Atlanta, however; in fact, he started his college career downright angry with Tech.

Defensive coordinator George O'Leary offered Page a scholarship, but then withdrew it because head coach Bill Lewis "wanted to go in another direction." As Page explained it, Lewis wanted "to wait on a recruit he had coming in the next weekend. I told him I wasn't going to sit around here and wait. I didn't like that very much."

So, thoroughly hacked off at Georgia Tech, Page accepted a scholarship offer from Howard Schnellenberger and Louisville. After Page's redshirt year, though, Schnellenberger left for Oklahoma, and Page started looking around. The fact that O'Leary was now the head coach at Tech intrigued him, though, he admitted, "I still had some hard feelings for Tech."

His respect for O'Leary and his desire to be a part of a better football program won out. He contacted O'Leary to see if he was interested; O'Leary was.

The player who was once angry at Georgia Tech eventually became its tenth All-American center.

Our society today is well aware of anger's destructive power because too many of us don't manage our anger as Craig Page did. Anger is a healthy component of a functional human being until – like other normal emotions such as fear, grief, and worry – it escalates out of control. Anger abounds on The Flats when Tech loses; the trouble comes when that anger intensifies from annoyance and disappointment to rage and destructive behavior.

Anger has both practical and spiritual consequences. Its great spiritual danger occurs when anger is "a purely selfish matter and the expression of a merely peevish vexation at unexpected and unwelcome misfortune or frustration" as when Tech fumbles at the Georgia five-yard line. It thus interferes with the living of the righteous, Christ-like life God intends for us.

Our own anger, therefore, can incur God's wrath; making God angry can never be anything but a perfectly horrendous idea.

When you get angry and start shouting, nothing good ever really happens.

--Olympic rower Michelle Guerette

**Anger becomes a problem when it escalates
into rage and interferes with the righteous life
God intends for us.**

DAY 82

WORM DROWNING

Read Mark 1:16-20.

"'Come, follow me,' Jesus said, 'and I will make you fishers of men'" (v. 17).

Tom Hammonds had only one problem with basketball: It kept him from his first love, which was bass fishing.

Hammonds is one of the greatest and the most popular players in Tech basketball history. He was a forward who many times played center from 1985-89.

Even playing out of position, he completed his career as only the third player in Tech history to score more than 2,000 points. He finished with 2,081 points and 885 rebounds, both fourth in Yellow Jacket history, and ended his career second only to Rick Yunkus in field goals made. Hammonds was All-ACC in both 1988 and '89 and third-team All-America in 1989. His jersey number (20) was retired during his senior season, and he was inducted into the Georgia Tech Hall of Fame in 1996.

Though Hammonds was fierce and determined on the court, he was laid back off it as his favorite hobby – bass fishing – revealed. "I really miss it," he said during his senior season. "Not just the fishing, but being out there on the lake by myself." Hammonds' other pursuits at Tech included his red pickup truck and regular attendance at tractor pulls.

Not surprisingly, he was a favorite of the Tech student body. On the night of his final home game, some students presented him with the "H" from the Tech Tower.

Hammonds was also a winner at Tech. He played on three teams that won 27, 22, and 20 games and on four teams that made it to the NCAA Tournament.

Perhaps you're like Tom Hammonds in that you're always looking for a chance to wet a hook. Think back to the worst fishing trip you ever had. You had a flat tire on the way. You got soaked and nearly froze. You didn't catch a thing. It was still better than a good day at work, wasn't it?

What if somebody in authority told you, "Go Fish"? How quickly would you trip over anybody who got in your way?

Well, somebody did give you that assignment. Jesus said go and fish for people who are drowning without him. Living in a society in which fishing was crucial to the livelihood of many and accompanied by disciples who had been professional fishermen, Jesus understood that fishing was a way of life for many and a passion for others.

"Go fish," he commanded, even to those who have never drowned a worm in their lives. And he meant it.

Some go to church and think about fishing; others go fishing and think about God.

-- Fisherman Tony Blake

Jesus understood the passion people have for fishing and commanded that it become not just a hobby but a way of life.

DAY 83

PEACEMONGERS

Read Hebrews 12:14-17.

"Make every effort to live in peace with all men and to be holy" (v. 14).

Like many Tech football players before and after him, Paul Duke suffered a broken bone on the turf of Grant Field. His break, however, occurred after his collegiate playing days were behind him.

Duke played for both William Alexander and Bobby Dodd. In 1945 he was Dodd's first captain, and he remembered the season as "a disaster. Seems like nothing went right." He returned in 1946 as a graduate student and was an All-American center. That season was much better with only two losses and a 41-19 win over St. Mary's in the Oil Bowl.

Duke played one year of pro football, and all the while he never suffered a broken bone. Then he came back to Atlanta for the Auburn game in 1948. Tech was winning easily at 27-0, and the Tigers weren't taking too kindly to the whipping. Play got increasingly physical, and Dodd put his regulars back in to regain control of the game in the fourth quarter. That didn't help much as play got rougher and rougher until finally a full-fledged brawl broke out.

Watching from the stands, Duke reacted without thinking. He jumped the fence and ran onto the field to help his former teammates. "Here I was squaring off with one player," he said, "when I got clobbered by another and suffered a broken nose. It was the first bone break I had ever suffered in football."

A night in Grady Hospital gave Duke time to think about what he had done. "I reflected on how foolish it was for a grown man with two children to be lying on his back with a broken nose," he said.

Perhaps you've never been in a brawl or a public brouhaha to match that of Paul Duke's and his Tech teammates. But maybe you retaliated when you got one elbow too many in a pickup basketball game. Or maybe you and your spouse or your teenager get into it occasionally, shouting and saying cruel things. Or road rage may be a part of your life.

While we do seem to live in a society that is more belligerent and confrontational than ever before, fighting is still not the way to solve a problem. Violence inevitably escalates the whole conflict, leaving wounded pride, intransigence, and simmering hatred in its wake. Actively seeking and making peace is the only way to a solution that lasts and heals.

Peacemaking is not as easy as fighting, but it is much more courageous and a lot less painful. It is also the Jesus thing to do.

No matter what the other fellow does on the field, don't let him lure you into a fight. Uphold your dignity.
-- Alabama Coach Frank Thomas

Making peace instead of fighting takes courage and strength, but it's certainly the less painful option.

A DOG'S LIFE

Read Genesis 6:11-22; 8:1-4.

"God remembered Noah and all the wild animals and the livestock that were with him in the ark" (v. 8:1).

For one season, Georgia Tech's mascot was – of all things -- a bulldog. Dogs also played a role in the recruiting of one of Tech's greatest basketball players.

For the 1905 football season, the official mascot of the Institute's football team was "a short-haired, square-jawed, real live bulldog." As the squad romped through its first seven games unscathed, it appeared Tech's athletic teams might very well be permanently known as the Bulldogs. State football history was changed forever, though, when a mediocre Sewanee team tied Tech 18-18. *The Atlanta Constitution* reported, "Tech's bulldog mascot became so sore at the end of the first half that he tore off his yellow and white streamers and went behind the grandstand to lick the daylights out of a sick cat."

After that upset, the bulldog garnered no more mentions as Tech's mascot. On Dec. 10, a small article in *The Atlanta Journal* mentioned the Yellow Jackets for the first time.

Tech basketball coach Whack Hyder had an unusual approach to recruiting Roger Kaiser. Every summer in the 1950s, Hyder loaded his family into the station wagon and headed north on recruiting trips. One Saturday afternoon in 1957, he pulled into the driveway of the Kaiser home in Dale, Ind. -- and sat in the car. Instead of immediately getting out and heading with a glad hand for the front porch where the Kaisers sat, Hyder let his two children spend five to ten minutes playing with the Kaiser family dogs before he left the station wagon.

The unorthodox approach worked as Kaiser, who would become the first All-America in Tech basketball history, decided right then to come to Atlanta.

Do you have a dog or two around the place? How about a cat? Kids have gerbils? Is it time to clean the tropical fish tank?

We share our living space with animals we pamper and protect as well as with some -- like roaches -- we seek to exterminate. None of us, though, has problems with our animals of the magnitude Noah did when he packed God's menagerie into one boat.

Noah built his floating zoo in response to God's concern for the survival of his creatures. God took care to preserve all his critters from extinction, including the fish, who were probably quite delighted with the whole flood business. The lesson we can draw from this is that all living things – not just mankind – are loved by God and are under his care.

It isn't just our pets that we're to care for and respect; it's all of God's creatures.

I like dogs better [than people]. With people, you never know which ones will bite.

-- *Diver Greg Louganis*

God cares about all his creatures, and he expects us to respect them too.

DAY 85

ROCK BOTTOM

Read Psalm 23.

"Even though I walk through the valley of the shadow of death, I will fear no evil for you are with me; your rod and your staff, they comfort me" (v. 4).

It's hard to believe now, but once upon a time the Georgia Tech volleyball program was the poster child for rock bottom.

The Jackets began volleyball competition in the ACC in 1983. Though the squad had a winning season in 1988, going 20-16, the team finished dead last in the conference for eight straight years. Even worse was that during that eight-year span of futility, the Jackets did not win a single ACC match. While other teams may have dreamed of top 20 rankings, the Jackets in 1990 were 8-30, 0-6 in the conference, and were ranked 248th.

The abysmal record rankled associate athletic director Bernadette McGlade, who determined to hire a first-rate coach and build a first-rate program. She reviewed more than one hundred applicants before hiring Shelton Collier because of his experience. When McGlade hired him, Collier was serving as an assistant with the U.S. women's national team.

Collier understandably realized he had a challenge on his hands when he arrived at The Flats in 1991. He knew the talent pool in Georgia wasn't that deep, but he also knew that with Tech's academic reputation he could recruit nationally. Collier promised a national ranking and an ACC title within five years.

He delivered.

His first year, Tech was 27-9, finally winning some ACC games. In 1994, the Jackets claimed their first-ever ACC title and established themselves as a perennial powerhouse. The beat continued when Bond Shymansky took over the program in 2002 and won 33 and 34 matches his first two seasons. Rock bottom is ancient history.

Maybe it was the day your business went under, taking everything you owned with it. Or the night your spouse walked out. Or the afternoon you learned your child was seriously, perhaps deathly, ill. You've known rock bottom.

Rock bottom is the time when life is its darkest. You are down in a dark valley looking up at the mountain peaks where the sun shines and people laugh and have hope. Rock bottom is the time when life is its loneliest, when "friends" and acquaintances desert you and the train wreck that is your life.

And yet in that darkness and that loneliness, you will find your best friend. You will find Jesus, who's been in that valley ahead of you. He knows sorrow, suffering, loss, and pain. Trust in him and he'll take you where he wound up after he walked through that valley; he'll take you all the way to glory.

Ain't nothing wrong with going down. It's staying down that's wrong.
-- Muhammad Ali

"Nobody knows what I'm going through!";
Jesus does because he's been there.

HOLLYWOOD ENDING

Read Luke 24:1-12.

"Why do you look for the living among the dead? He is not here; he has risen!" (vv. 5, 6a)

What Tech quarterback Gary Lanier did on Nov. 6, 1976, and how he got there are too far-fetched even for Hollywood's overly imaginative script writers to dream up.

When Lanier arrived at Tech in August 1976, he was the fourth-string quarterback who hoped to make the traveling squad. But Coach Pepper Rodgers' triple-option offense was rough on quarterbacks. Three went down, leaving only Lanier, who said Rodgers looked at him and took a deep breath "like he was saying to himself, 'Either put in Lanier or fold.'" He put in Lanier, who wasn't necessarily exceptional. After a loss to Duke, Rodgers took the blame for the defeat by telling Lanier, "I should never have had a quarterback of your abilities out there."

The question thus was how badly the 3-4-1 Jackets would lose to 11th-ranked Notre Dame. But when Lanier was sacked on the game's second play, Rodgers made a decision that resulted in one of the oddest wins in Tech history. He told Lanier, "I'm not calling another pass play." "That's fine with me," Lanier replied.

Notre Dame jumped out to a 14-3 lead, but then the Hollywood story tossed all sense of reason and logic out the window. The fourth-string freshman quarterback led the Jackets to a 23-14 win without attempting a single pass, as Rodgers had promised.

"Of all the quarterbacks who have beaten Notre Dame, Lanier was the worst," Rodgers said afterwards. Lanier laughed. He knew he was already a part of Tech lore: the quarterback who beat Notre Dame without throwing a pass and the hero in a story so downright wacky even Hollywood couldn't dream it up.

The world tells us that happy endings are for fairy tales and the movies, that reality is Cinderella dying in childbirth and her prince getting killed in a peasant uprising. But that's just another of the world's lies.

The truth is that Jesus Christ has been producing happy endings for almost two millennia. That's because in Jesus lies the power to change and to rescue a life no matter how desperate the situation. Jesus is the master at putting shattered lives back together, of healing broken hearts and broken relationships, of resurrecting lost dreams.

And as for living happily ever after – God really means it. The greatest Hollywood ending of them all was written on a Sunday morning centuries ago when Jesus left a tomb and death behind. With faith in Jesus, your life can have that same ending. You live with God in peace, joy, and love – forever. The End.

This field, this game, is a part of our past, Ray. It reminds us of all that once was good, and that could be again.
-- James Earl Jones in Field of Dreams

Hollywood's happy endings are products
of imagination; the happy endings Jesus produces
are real and are yours for the asking.

DAY 87

BRAGGING RIGHTS

Read Job 38.

"Have you ever given orders to the morning, or shown the dawn its place?" (v. 12)

It's difficult to imagine a Georgia Tech football game in which the Rambling Wreck doesn't lead the team onto Grant Field, but officially the tradition didn't begin until 1961.

The term "Rambling Wreck" was first applied to a 1914 Ford owned by Tech's Dean of Men, Floyd Field. Censure from the Tech student newspaper in 1927 didn't keep Field from trading the car away.

Beginning in 1929, the newspaper kept the tradition alive – albeit loosely – by sponsoring annual auto races from Atlanta to Athens. These eventually were discontinued when they became increasingly dangerous. In their place is Homecoming's Rambling Wreck Parade, which "challenges students to produce outlandish 'mechanical monstrosities' capable of traversing a short course on campus."

In the late 1950s, school officials decided a return to the "Rambling Wreck" tradition was needed. Dean of Students James Dull searched for a pre-1940 vintage model and found one – parked in front of his own apartment building. The owner was Capt. Ted Johnson, a Delta pilot, who had recently finished restoring the 1930 Ford Cabriolet sport coupe. Johnson intended to give the car to his son but decided to let Tech have it for $1,000 in May 1961. He later returned the purchase price to the school, thus completing the donation of the car to the Institute.

On Sept. 30, 1961, against Rice, the official Rambling Wreck for the first time led the Yellow Jackets onto the stadium turf. Tech won 24-0. The car has been a fixture at Tech home games ever since.

While we are fond of the Rambling Wreck, we sure wouldn't want to take her down I-75. We'd much prefer contemporary cars for serious traveling. Our cars are impressive, even if they will one day – like the Rambling Wreck – be superseded by superior technology.

Mankind is forever busy with his achievements and his progress. Cars, planes, computers, Ipods, Double Stuf Oreos. We have been to the moon, virtually eliminated polio, built a tunnel from England to France, concocted weapons capable of destroying our planet, and invented the flush toilet and Velcro.

The truth is, though, that we are nothing compared to God. We brag about space flight; God fashioned the moon, the planets, and the stars and hung them in the heavens he created. Man conducts a symphony; God directs the dawn. Man feebly predicts the weather; God commands it.

In truth, we have little of which to boast except that God loves us. Now that's worth bragging about!

Let the competition begin; let the glory be God's.
-- from the Fellowship of Christian Athletes Competitor's Creed

**Boasting and bragging about ourselves
and our accomplishments is one sure way
to make God laugh.**

DAY 88

PLAYING BY THE RULES

Read Luke 6:1-11.

"They were furious and began to discuss with one another what they might do to Jesus" (v. 11).

No soap and hot water. No pork or pastry.

Those were among the rules legendary coach John Heisman had for his football players. Heisman coached on The Flats from 1904 to 1919 with a 102-29-7 record that included four undefeated teams and the 1917 national champions.

He also revolutionized college football; he is credited with bringing the forward pass to the game and inventing the shotgun snap. He was the first coach to use yardage marker and uniform numbers and the first to instruct the scoreboard operator to post down and distance before each play.

Nevertheless, Heisman was an eccentric who coached with a strict set of rules unimaginable in today's wide-open game. He decreed that no two end runs should ever be run in succession and no pass should be thrown within 30 yards of the Tech goal. His teams were to punt on first down if they were close to their own goal. "When in doubt, punt anyway, anywhere," he declared. Tech players lived by his 175 axioms of play, which included "Don't have your feet in the way of the snapback"; "Don't forget to stiff-arm"; "Don't look toward where the play is going"; and "Don't go into the line with your head up."

His rules went far beyond mere game planning. (See aforementioned hot water and pork.) He drew up twenty-one dietary restrictions for his players, some of which were totally arbitrary. For instance, he approved of all vegetables except cabbage and insisted his players eat only stale or toasted bread.

Like Heisman's players, you live by rules others set up. Some lender decided how much interest you pay on your mortgage and your car loan. You work hours and shifts somebody else set up. Someone else decided what day your garbage gets picked up.

Societies in general, though, are able to function because of rules that are generally observed; without them we would have only chaos. Try driving without any rules of the road.

Sometimes, however, society imposes rules that like some of Heisman's seem purely arbitrary. For instance, Jesus encountered societal rules that told him what company he should keep. He flaunted them, choosing love instead of the rules and mingling freely with society's outcasts.

You, too, have to choose when you find yourself in the presence of someone whom society says is undesirable. Will you choose disdain or love? Are you willing to be a rebel for love — as Jesus was?

I believe in rules. Sure I do. If there weren't any rules, how could you break them?

-- Leo Durocher

Society's rules dictate who is acceptable and who is not, but love in the name of Jesus knows no such distinctions.

A LONG SHOT

Read Matthew 9:9-13.

"[Jesus] saw a man named Matthew sitting at the tax collector's booth. 'Follow me,' he told him, and Matthew got up and followed him" (v. 9).

You would think a tennis player who won Georgia Tech's first-ever NCAA singles title, set a school record for wins in a season (45), and helped her team to a national championship would be one of the most highly recruited and publicized players in the country. If you're talking about Amanda McDowell, you would be wrong.

McDowell was a long shot for such sensational success when she arrived at Tech in 2006. She was so unheralded coming out of Atlanta's Marist High that she had to fight to even get a spot on the squad. That team was pretty good, though; they were the 2007 NCAA national champions. She wound up at no. 4 singles for the champs and won 6-1, 6-0 in the national championship match against UCLA. Still, McDowell had a long way to go to be in the mix for a singles title. She finished her freshman season ranked 90th in the nation.

But in 2008, she kept getting better as a sophomore, continuing the journey from obscurity to national fame. She played most of the season at no. 2 singles and improved her ranking to no. 7 in the country. She closed the season by winning her last 15 matches.

Then in the NCAA singles tournament in Tulsa, McDowell

survived a first-round match that saw her lose the first set 6-1 and overcome four match points in the second set. In the finals, she defeated the 2005 champion 6-2, 6-3.

Amanda McDowell was a long shot no more. She was now the favorite.

Matthew the tax collector was another long shot, an unlikely person to be a confidant of the Son of God. While we may not get all warm and fuzzy about the IRS, our government's revenue agents are nothing like Matthew and his ilk. He bought a franchise, paying the Roman Empire for the privilege of extorting, bullying, and stealing everything he could from his own people. Tax collectors of the time were "despicable, vile, unprincipled scoundrels."

And yet, Jesus said only two words to this lowlife: "Follow me." Jesus knew that this long shot would make an excellent disciple.

It's the same with us. While we may not be quite as vile as Matthew was, none of us can stand before God with our hands clean and our hearts pure. We are all impossibly long shots to enter God's Heaven. That is, until we do what Matthew did: get up and follow Jesus.

Overcoming challenges should never be considered a long shot.
-- Mother of disabled child on MightyMikeBasketball.com

Only through Jesus does our status change
from being long shots to enter God's Kingdom
to being heavy favorites.

CELEBRATION TIME

Read Exodus 14:26-31; 15:19-21.

"Miriam the prophetess, Aaron's sister, took a tambourine in her hand, and all the women followed her, with tambourines and dancing" (v. 15:20).

Scott Sisson's foot touched of a celebration the likes of which Georgia Tech had not seen for decades.

With only seven seconds left to play, Sisson booted a 37-yard field goal that lifted the Jackets to a 41-38 win over top-ranked Virginia in Charlottesville on Nov. 3, 1990. With that kick, Tech became a national title contender.

The celebration in the locker room after the game was as wild and as exuberant as could be expected. The team was "ankle deep in tears and sodas" by the time they left for Atlanta. On the flight home, players and coaches danced in the aisles; several hundred fans greeted them at the airport.

But all that was only a prelude for the real thing.

The players were used to returning to campus anonymously, so they didn't really expect anything else. When he saw a roadblock and dozens of police officers, quarterback Shawn Jones "thought there was a fight or something." And then the buses turned onto Techwood Drive – and what greeted them were thousands and thousands of Tech fans and students.

"Wall-to-wall people, and madness, hysteria," said guard Jim Lavin. Jack Wilkinson wrote, "Fans cheered players, hugged them, slapped their backs, shook their hands, kissed them, got their autographs." The fans – old and young alike – set a "bonfire of the insanities" and tore down both Grant Field goal posts.

"It was as if we had just won the Super Bowl," said fullback William Bell of the celebration, which, as the season unfolded, was exactly what Tech had done collegiately.

Invite some friends over, turn the game on TV, fire up the grill, pull out the salsa and chips, and you've got a party. Any excuse for a celebration will do; all you really need is a sense that life is pretty good right now.

But the party ends. The coals cool to ash, the burgers are all devoured, the friends go home, and you wearily face the dreary prospect of cleaning up the remains. What if, however, the spontaneous joy of a party weren't temporary; what if your entire life were lived in that attitude of almost reckless celebration?

Jesus offers that chance because he turns all of life into a celebration of the good life. Tragedies and setbacks will come, but the heart given to Jesus will find the joy in living no matter what. The party never stops when a life is celebrated with Jesus because every day is a celebration of victory.

What are all these people doing?
  – Offensive lineman Mike Mooney on the crowds that met the team
  buses after the Virginia win

**With Jesus, life is one big party, a celebration
of victory and joy.**

NOTES
(by Devotional Day Number)

1   "no gate, no crowds [and] little interest.": Al Thomy, *The Ramblin' Wreck* (Huntsville, AL: The Strode Publishers, 1973), p. 30.

1   While local newspapers ignored the event,: Thomy, p. 18.

1   He generally is credited with . . . tradition were planted,": Thomy, p. 19.

2   Bear Bryant called Dodd . . . the smartest coach he'd ever known.: Adam Van Brimmer, *Stadium Stories: Georgia Tech Yellow Jackets* (Guilford, CN: The Globe Pequot Press, 2006), p. 43.

2   "discarded all . . . toil and heavy work": Thomy, p. 148.

2   practices that were short, . . . volleyball on Friday.: Van Brimmer, *Stadium Stories,* p. 34.

2   "I want my players to enjoy the game,": Thomy, p. 149.

2   "used methods that . . . go to church every Sunday.: Thomy, p. 149.

2   I think God made it simple. Just accept him and believe.: Jim and Julie S. Bettinger, *The Book of Bowden* (Nashville: TowleHouse Publishing, 2001), p. 47.

3   Most publications predicted . . . seventh in the ACC.: Patrice Lomax, "The Team That Bee-Lieved," *Georgia Tech: 2008-09 Basketball Media Guide,* p. 174, http://grfx.cstv.com/photos/schools/geot/sports/m-baskbl/auto_pdf/0809-m-baskbl-mg-9.pdf.

3   The key to the season was the continuous growth of the players.: Lomax.

3   In the NCAA Tournament, . . . past Oklahoma State 67-65: "Tech Basketball Heritage," *Georgia Tech: 2008-09 Basketball Media Guide,* p. 123, http://grfx.cstv.com/photos/schools/geot/sports/m-baskbl/auto_pdf/0809-m-baskbl-mg-9.pdf.

4   "We're not that good . . . not meant to win.": Jack Wilkinson, *Focused on the Top* (Atlanta: Longstreet Press, 1991), p. 16.

4   On the Monday following . . . what you want to do,": Wilkinson, p. 18.

4   If they weren't willing . . . I was dead serious": Wilkinson, pp. 18, 20.

4   Senior noseguard Jeff Mathis spoke . . . with Ross and his staff.: Wilkinson, p. 20.

4   "From that moment on, . . . That moment was the turnaround.": Wilkinson, p. 21.

5   Freshman Wade Mitchell, who took over . . . no holding them back.": Thomy, p. 203.

6   left Coach Shelton Collier considering . . . and we have to win.": Ailene Voisin, "Tech Stays on Road to Volleyball Elite," *The Atlanta Journal-Constitution,* Sept. 26, 1995, http://us.mg2.mail.yahoo.com/dc/launch?.rand=avq5k0inu277j, Nov. 24, 2008.

7   "He just got better as the game progressed.": Charles Aldinger, "Liberty Bowl 1972: Georgia Tech Iowa State," http://www.mmbolding.com/bowls/Liberty_1972.htm, Nov. 19, 2008.

7   "It was just fantastic. . . . Jim Stevens do great?": Aldinger.

8   Atlanta's many theaters . . . chances for stage performances.: Thomy, p.

35.

8   Heisman invited the athletic board . . . to remain in Atlanta.": Thomy, pp. 82-83.

8   "'Embarrassed and flabbergasted" . . . news to the press.": Thomy, p. 83.

9   Shortly after King started, . . . double-breasted, 1940s suit.: Kim King with Jack Wilkinson, *Kim King's Tales from the Georgia Tech Sideline* (Champaign, IL: Sports Publishing L.L.C., 2004), pp. 156-57.

10   Rushed to a hospital emergency . . . injury healed without it,: Mike Knobler, "Ready for Action," *The Atlanta Journal-Constitution*, June 3, 2005, p. D1, http://us.mg2mmail.yahoo.com/dc/launch?.gx=1&. rand=aj5tp61nsg1vj, Jan. 15, 2009.

10   The only lingering evidence . . . "I'm counting my blessings,": Knobler, "Ready for Action."

11   left "in his wake a series . . . I had great coverage!": Austin Murphy, "Hands Down," *Sports Illustrated*, Oct. 23, 2006, http://vault.sportsillustrated.cnn.com/vault/article/magazine/MAG1113320/index.htm, Sept. 15, 2008.

11   "He always had a kind . . . things will work out.": Murphy.

11   during the summer of 2006 . . . less fortunate than he.: "Calvin Johnson (American Football)," *Wikipedia, the free encyclopedia*, http://en.wikipedia.org/wiki/Calvin_Johnson_ (football), Nov. 24, 2008.

12   The media had already . . . team in the nation.: Van Brimmer, pp. 25-26.

12   "I will give you a plan . . . win their three games." Thomy, p. 117.

12   The rest of the squad . . . "The plan cannot fail,": Thomy, p. 118.

12   Alexander "didn't miss a trick.": Thomy, p. 119.

13   scored 26 straight points against them in the last half: Carter Strickland, "Mitchell Outburst Rallied Jackets, *The Atlanta Journal-Constitution*, March 17, 2007, http://us.mg2.mail.yahoo.com/dc/launch?.rand=av15k0inu277j, Nov. 24, 2008.

13   In the locker room after the game, . . . rallied around her and agreed,": Strickland.

14   "a lot of fun,": Wilkinson, p. 81.

14   many Jackets on the sideline couldn't watch.: Wilkinson, p, 85.

15   an off-tackle run. . . . instead of a forward pass.": Thomy, p. 31.

15   After his senior year in 1903, . . . to John Heisman of Clemson.: Thomy, p. 31.

15   "Boom-a-lacka, Boom-a-lacka, . . . Georgia School of Technology.": Thomy, p. 29.

16   because the games weren't played . . . hall on Broad Street.: Bill Ballew, *Yellow Jackets Handbook* (Wichita, KS: The Wichita Eagle and Beacon Publishing Co., 1996), p. 7.

16   The old school foundry . . . first-ever on-campus game.: Ballew, p. 8.

16   The program lapsed again . . . around the city.: Ballew, p. 9.

16   In October 1923, athletic director . . . time for the 1934-35 season.: Ballew, p. 10.

16   a bandbox that seated fewer than 1,800,: Ballew, p. 12.

17   "rode a motorcycle to the office . . . permed his hair.":

	Van Brimmer, *Stadium Stories*, p. 106.
17	As Rodgers' mother, Louise, . . . hair the next day.": Van Brimmer, p. 106.
18	Jones set a school record by averaging 16.4 yards per carry: Larry Hartstein, "Chamblee High's Jones Run Wild for Tech," *ajc.com*, http://www.ajc.com/sprots/content/sports/gatech/stories/2008/11/29/georgia_tech_roddy, Nov. 30, 2008.
18	"Hey, it's sixty minutes. . . . it'd be on one play,": Thomas Stinson, "Georgia Tech Storms Past Georgia," *ajc.com*, http://www/ajc.com/sprots/content/sports/gatech/stories/2008/11/29/tech_georgia, Nov. 30, 2008.
19	Only, Hamilton was 30 . . . took years of overtime,": Mike Knobler, "Star Athletes Joe Hamilton, Brian Oliver Back at Ga. Tech to Finally Score Diplomas," *The Atlanta Journal-Constitution*, Aug. 3, 2007, http://us.mg2.mail.yahoo.com/dc/launch?.rand=avq5k0inu277j, Nov. 24, 2008.
19	Oliver eventually played basketball . . . but nobody like this,": Knobler, "Star Athletes."
20	repeatedly telling her . . . into a national champion.: Carter Strickland, "Shelton's Jackets Climb to Top," *The Atlanta Journal-Constitution*, May 23, 2007, http://us.mg2.mail.yahoo.com/dc/launch?.rand=av15k0inu277j, Nov. 24, 2008.
20	"It has been an unbelievable . . . an amazing accomplishment.": Strickland, "Shelton's Jackets."
20	"I have never seen Ally . . . She always comes through.": Strickland, "Shelton's Jackets."
21	"We were so dead in the water.": Ballew, p. 59.
21	"We knew going into . . . and I mean hammered,": Ballew, p. 59.
21	"just as things appeared . . . rose from the grave.": Ballew, p. 59.
21	Point guard Stephon Marbury said . . . told you you're crazy,": Ballew, p. 59.
21	"I'll never forget this team,": Ballew, p. 61.
22	"Clint Castleberry could have . . . the South has produced,": Thomy, p. 142.
22	Castleberry's No. 19 . . . Georgia Tech's football history: "Retired Jersey #19: Clint Castleberry, RB," *Georgia Tech Football: The Perfect Option: 2008 Media Guide*, http://ramblinwreck.cstv.com/sports/m-football/spec-rel/08-fb-media-guide.html, p. 155.
22	"blazed across the field . . . on his way to South Bend.: "Retired Jersey #19."
22	"That was a thing of beauty, . . . all kicks on the run.": Thomy, p. 143.
22	"He was a star . . . and then he was gone,": Thomy, p. 143.
22	No one knows when . . . blink of an eye.: Bettinger, p. 21.
23	The players stood around . . . ball was still in play.: John E. Stegeman, *The Ghosts of Herty Field* (Athens: The University of Georgia Press, 1997), p. 72.
23	"Suddenly both elevens . . . yanked back by some rival.": Stegeman, p. 72.
23	Tech's Red Wilson used a stump to propel himself: Thomy, p. 40.
23	with a Georgia player . . . roll across the battlefield.": Stegeman, pp. 72-73.

184

24   "That's the kind of stuff . . . the guys "keep battling."": D. Orlando Ledbetter, "Jackets Rally Again to Win ACC Title," *The Atlanta Journal-Constitution*, May 30, 2005, p. B1, http://us.mg2.mail.yahoo.com/dc/launch?.
gx=1&.rand=5jipv0jogmina, Jan. 14, 2009.

25   "the toughest four days of my life.": Thomy, p. 198.

25   Van Leer, Coach Bobby Dodd, and other . . . teams for several seasons.:
Thomy, p. 197.

25   Gov. Marvin Griffin expressed . . . could play the game.: Thomy, p. 198.

25   Six weeks after his showdown . . . died of a cerebral hemorrhage.:
Thomy, p. 198.

25   I won't tolerate a womanizer, . . . cost you your job.: Bettinger, p. 26.

26   The Tech band was founded . . . until he graduated in 1912.: "Georgia
Tech Yellow Jacket Marching Band," *Wikipedia, the free encyclopedia*,
http:///en.wikipedia.org/wiki/Georgia_Tech_Athletic_Bands, Sept. 17,
2008.

26   Mike Greenblatt followed him . . . female members of the band.: "Georgia Tech Bands: Music Department History," http://gtband.net/joomla/
index.php?option=com_content&task=view&id=65&Itemid=87, Sept. 12,
2008.

26   The Tech band pulled off . . . boos from the home crowd,": "Georgia
Tech Yellow Jacket Marching Band."

27   the Jackets proved miracles work both ways.: John Chandler Griffin,
Georgia vs. Georgia Tech (Athens: Hill Street Press, 2000), p. 295.

28   In an idle conversation with . . . a net back to you.": Thomas Stinson,
Georgia Tech's Lethal Weapons, (Savannah: Golden Coast Publishing Co.,
1990), p. 45.

28   which he wore around his neck . . . left the locker room.: Stinson,
Georgia Tech's Lethal Weapons, p. 51.

29   In the late 1950s, . . . he should play elsewhere,": Thomy, p. 208.

29   Asked before the game . . . the devil out of them.": Thomy, p. 209.

29   A 32-yard Dodd Jr. pass . . . on the pads or cry.": Thomy, p. 210.

30   he went to Coach Bobby Ross . . . deep return man: Wilkinson, p. 53.

30   Tisdel was not on the dress list for the Duke game.: Wilkinson, p. 67.

30   Tisdel told his parents he was through.: Wilkinson, p. 68.

30   In the locker room, . . . before he did anything.: Wilkinson, p. 67.

30   Ross immediately noticed . . . he was returning kickoffs.: Wilkinson, p.
68.

30   breaking seven tackles: Wilkinson, p. 68.

30   Ross announced that Kevin Tisdale now had a scholarship.: Wilkinson,
p. 69.

31   "She's 5-[foot]-6 with . . . 55-54 win over DePaul.: Mike Knobler,
"Jackets Duo Making Thievery Pay Off Big," *The Atlanta Journal-
Constitution*, March 22, 2008, http://us.mg2.mail.yahoo.com/dc/launch?.
rand=avq5k0inu277j, Nov. 24, 2008.

32   Many of those who gathered . . . expected a bloodbath.: Morton
Shamik and Robert Creamer, "A Rough Day for the Bear," *Sports
Illustrated*, Nov. 26, 1962, http://vault.sportsillustrated.
cnn.com/vault/article/magazine/MAG1074338/index.htm,

32 Sept. 15, 2008.
    "in an unnecessary block . . . referee's whistle had sounded.": Shamik and Cramer.

32 Tech fans, faculty, and alumni . . . relations after the 1964 game.: Shamik and Creamer.

32 "I believe that was the cleanest . . . expect anything different.": Shamik and Creamer.

33 "Perhaps no one in . . . a greater program builder.": Barry Jacobs, "One of a Kind," *Georgia Tech: 2008-90 Basketball Media Guide*, p. 196, http://grfx.cstv.com/photos/schools/geot/sports/m-baskbl/auto_pdf/0809-m-baskbl-mg-9.pdf.

33 "I've got to give those two . . very, very special people.": Thomas Stinson, "The Start of Something Good," *Georgia Tech: 2008-09 Basketball Media Guide*, p. 188, http://grfx.cstv.com/photos/schools/geot/sports/m-baskbl/auto_pdf/0809-m-baskbl-mg-9.pdf.

33 Bruce Dalrymple and Duane Ferrell . . . to symbolize Tech basketball.": Stinson, "The Start of Something Good," p. 189.

33 they met for the first time . . . Tech's return to grace.": Stinson, "The Start of Something Good," p. 188.

33 "We do not choose . . . on which we will stand.": R. Alan Culpepper, "The Gospel of Luke: Introduction, Commentary, and Reflections," *The New Interpreter's Bible* (Nashville: Abingdon Press, 1995), Vol. IX, p. 153.

34 Heisman insisted he broke . . . wins over strong opponents.: Van Brimmer, *Stadium Stories*, p. 11.

34 Heisman had held a grudge . . . buddies to play the game.: Van Brimmer, *Stadium Stories*, pp. 11-12.

34 You're doing all right . . . up their sleeves.: Van Brimmer, *Stadium Stories*, p. 12.

35 defensive end Darrell Robertson . . . supplement and not a food.: Mike Knobler, "Dietitian Tips the Scales in Yellow Jackets' Favor," *The Atlanta Journal-Constitution*, Sept. 8, 2006, http://us.mg2.mail.yahoo.com/dc/launch?.rand=avq5k0inu277j, Nov. 24, 2008.

36 Bobby Kimmel hadn't even expected . . . he was on scholarship.: Ballew, p. 79.

36 With 1:12 left, Kimmel . . . he forced a turnover: Ballew, pp. 78-79.

36 I had a good alibi . . . and win the game.: Bettinger, p. 116.

37 "It would be good to start off with a win.": Thomy, p. 91.

37 "a runner of power and speed," . . . the next four games.: Thomy, p. 91.

37 "in the light snow of the Steel City,": Thomy, p. 93.

37 The talk – even in . . . injury the Saturday before.: Thomy, p. 93.

37 "his teeth were lashed . . . without anaesthetic.": Thomy, p. 93.

38 "You run one more play, . . . five yards closer.": King, p. 130.

39 The California native came east . . . I really CAN jump over the stick.": Andy Holt, "Ramblin' with Chaunte Howard, *Technique*, Sept. 10, 2004, http://dev.nique.gatech.edu/issues/2004-09-10/sports, Nov. 2, 2008.

40 "It was the coldest I'd ever been,": Van Brimmer, *Stadium Stories*, p. 118.

40 The snow was so thick . . . twice before kickoff.: David Davidson, "NCAA Rushing Record," *Georgia Tech Football: The Perfect Option: 2008*

Media Guide, p. 152, http://ramblinwreck.cstv.com/sports/m-football/spec-rel/08-fb-media-guide.html.

40   As he went out for warm-ups, . . . than cleated shoes.": Van Brimmer, *Stadium Stories*, pp. 118-19.

40   The combination of eggs, . . . force-fed him Pepto-Bismol.: Van Brimmer, *Stadium Stories*, p. 119.

40   As he neared the record . . . until he got the record.: Davidson.

40   It's amazing! . . . to be a Christian man.: Bettinger, p. 121.

41   Dodd had chafed . . . Tech's withdrawal from the SEC.: Van Brimmer, *Stadium Stories*, p. 92.

42   In a game against Florida State . . . you never do it,": John Hollis, "Disease Can't Derail Desire," *The Atlanta Journal-Constitution*, June 9, 2004, p. E1, http://us.mg2.mail.yahoo.com/dc/launch?.gx=1&.rand=3rl2d803lim74, Jan. 23, 2009.

42   He once said that when . . . in Trapani's mid-30s.: Hollis, "Disease Can't Derail Desire."

43   When Kaiser arrived in town, . . . am I doing here?": Stinson, *Georgia Tech's Lethal Weapons*, p. 12.

43   "was a landmark in Tech history.": Stinson, *Georgia Tech's Lethal Weapons*, p. 12.

43   Kaiser scored 26 of Tech's last 23 points: Stinson, *Georgia Tech's Lethal Weapons*, p. 12.

44   The helmet was a piece . . . provided them himself.: Clyde Bolton, *The Crimson Tide* (Huntsville, AL: The Strode Publishers, 1972), p. 46.

44   Hiding the ball under a jersey.: Clyde Bolton, *War Eagle* (Huntsville, AL: The Strode Publishers, 1973), p. 69.

44   Using a helmet for a kicking tee.: Bolton, *War Eagle*, p. 78.

44   Spectators rushing . . . in the players' way.: Bolton, *War Eagle*, p. 49.

44   Players dragging ball carriers forward.: Bolton, *War Eagle*, p. 76.

44   Linemen holding hands . . . before a play began.: Bolton, *The Crimson Tide*, p. 47.

44   Darkness forcing games to be called.: Bolton, *War Eagle*, p. 48.

44   Teams deciding upon . . . once they showed up.: Bolton, *War Eagle*, p. 80.

44   when handles were sewn . . . easier to toss.: Bolton, *War Eagle*, p. 76.

45   "I get on an elevator, and it's me and five guys,": Michelle Hiskey, "A Cheerful Bequest," *The Atlanta Journal-Constitution*, Feb. 27, 2005, p. D1, http://us.mg2.mail.yahoo.com/dc/launch?.gx=1&.rand=3rl2d803lim74, Jan. 13, 2009.

45   She had no intentions . . . scholarships for high-school cheerleaders.: Hiskey.

46   His picture with movie star . . . . the Atlanta papers.; Thomy, p. 125.

46   After the game, fullback . . . back to the Tech campus.: Van Brimmer, *Stadium Stories*, p. 25.

46   Thomason donated him to the Buffalo zoo.: Thomy, p. 132.

46   That's just Stumpy's bear. . . . he'll go home.: Thomy, p. 132.

47   Tech crossed the fifty-yard . . . once the entire game.: Bill Cromartie, *Clean Old-Fashioned Hate* (Huntsville, AL: The Strode Publishers, 1977), p. 212.

47   "the old Vol waiting game, . . . waiting for a break.": Cromartie, p. 214.

47   Tech didn't even have . . . 18 total yards,: Cromartie, p. 214.

48   "Told you so," free safety . . . the 1990 Georgia game: Wilkinson, p. 2.

48   "had less lofty aims than many . . . happy with a 7-4 season.: Wilkinson, p. 28.

48   On Tech's Media Day . . . a young man talking.": Wilkinson, p. 29.

49   "He was the X factor,": "soaking up knowledge.": Matt Winkeljohn, "Valuable Role Player Learning a New Role," *The Atlanta Journal-Constitution*, Dec. 27, 2007, http://us.mg2.mail.yahoo.com/dc/launch?.rand=avq5k0inu277j, Nov. 24, 2008.

50   he needed six years . . . so he could letter.: Van Brimmer, *Stadium Stories*, p. 28.

50   Knute Rockne once remarked . . . any coach in America.": Van Brimmer, *Stadium Stories*, p. 22.

51   Alexandra Preiss' sense of adventure . . . as a volleyball player,": Wendy Parker, "Has Game, Will Travel (Quite Far)," *The Atlanta Journal-Constitution*, Dec. 11, 2003, http://us.mg2.mail.yahoo.com/dc/launch?.rand=avq5k0inu277j, Nov. 24, 2008.

51   "It wouldn't have surprised . . . Taco Bell.: Parker, "Have Game."

52   He called Dennis Scott and other . . . who made it to San Antonio: Tony Barnhart, "The Final Four: Glow Spans Different Eras," *The Atlanta Journal-Constitution*, April 1, 2004, http://us.mg2.mail.yahoo.com/dc/launch?.rand=avq5k0inu277j, Nov. 24, 2008.

53   "Our dads decided we were going to Georgia Tech,": Katie B. Davis, "Pictures of the Past: From Birth to Earth," *The Gainesville Times*, July 9, 2008, http://www.gainesvilletimes.com/news/archive/6895, Jan. 20, 2009.

53   "We've done everything in our lives . . . Martin was among the pall-bearers.: Davis.

54   In 1949, Coach Bobby Dodd got . . . sneaked in from the one.: Adam Van Brimmer, "Tech Heroes Born in 'Drought Years,'" *The Augusta Chronicle*, Nov. 22, 2007, http://chronicle.augusta.com/stories/112207/gat_153435.shtml, Nov. 4, 2008.

54   In 1950, the drought maker was . . . run by Darrell Crawford.: Van Brimmer, *Stadium Stories*, p. 76.

54   quarterback Wade Mitchell, was three . . . momentum-swinging tackle in 1955,: Van Brimmer, *Stadium Stories*, pp. 82-83.

55   In Paul Johnson's hometown . . . instead of a red suit.": Mike Knobler, "Excellence Required," *The Atlanta Journal-Constitution*, Dec. 16, 2007, http://us.mg2.mail.yahoo.com/dc/launch?.rand=avq5k0inu277j, Nov. 24, 2008.

55   "There might be mornings . . . I can from 8 to 1.": Knobler, "Excellence Required."

55   When he was 12, . . . as a golf caddie.: Knobler, "Excellence Required."

55   Johnson was a perfect fit . . . if it plays smart.": Mark Bradley, "Captain Sees His Old Ship Sail True," *The Atlanta Journal-Constitution*, Dec. 2, 2008, http://www.ajc.com/sports/content/printedition/2008.12/02/bradley.html, Dec. 17, 2008.

56   "help get Tech basketball back where it belongs": "Harping on Har-

pring," *Georgia Tech: 2008-09 Basketball Media Guide*, p. 191, http://grfx.cstv.com/photos/schools/geot/sports/m-baskbl/auto_pdf/0809-m-baskbl-mg-9.pdf.

56   with just over a minute left, . . . a huge honor and compliment.": "Harping on Harpring."

57   Thirty-three thousand fans . . . a Southern football game,: ": Cromartie, p. 93.

57   The Yellow Jackets moved to . . . strategy had Tech employed?": Cromartie, p. 96.

58   Cremins was just looking . . . we were doing a good job.": Susan Howard, "Taking It to the Hoop," *The Atlanta Journal-Constitution*, Nov. 17, 1985, http://us.mg2.mail.yahoo.com/dc/launch?.rand=avq5k0inu277j, Nov. 24, 2008.

58   "He made himself a player . . . never be a good ball player.: Howard.

58   You have to listen . . . for a way to improve.: Freeman, Criswell, ed., *The Wisdom of Southern Football* (Nashville: Walnut Grove Press, 1995), p. 110.

59   "the most depressing thing I ever had to do": Van Brimmer, *Stadium Stories*, p. 47.

59   Dodd considering resigning.: Van Brimmer, *Stadium Stories*, p. 46.

59   "Six seasons into what . . . football team peaked.": Van Brimmer, *Stadium Stories*, p. 46.

59   Guard George Morris compared . . . his to Rose Bowl field.: Van Brimmer, *Stadium Stories*, p. 48.

59   "spring of desperation.": Van Brimmer, *Stadium Stories*, Stadium Stories, p. 46.

59   "The sun came out.": Van Brimmer, *Stadium Stories*, p. 49.

60   Tech's band members "arose . . . to rattle Georgia's pitcher.: Griffin, p. 55.

60   The Tech "stunt" . . . the order of the day": Cromartie, pp. 86-87.

60   including quite a few fist fights.: Griffin, p. 56.

60   "The old enemies joined hands . . . Kaiser should be hung.": Griffin, p. 56.

61   Homer Rice was on vacation . . . had bolted for Alabama.: Wilkinson, p. 3.

61   Rice knew he had to find . . . go ahead and recommend you.": Wilkinson, p. 5.

61   Rice persuaded Ross to fly . . . The vote was unanimous;: Wilkinson, p. 6.

62   Lever grew up in Buffalo, . . . from the beginning of time,": Matt Winkeljohn, "Built of Fire and Ice," *The Atlanta Journal-Constitution*, May 9, 2007, p. D1. http://us.mg2.mail.yahoo.com/dc/launch?.gx=1&.rand=3rl2d803lim74, Jan. 13, 2009.

62   Lever never realized his dream . . . from home to mature some.": Winkeljohn, "Built of Fire and Ice."

62   "She's definitely the best every-day player I've ever had,": Winkeljohn, "Built of Fire and Ice."

63   On the night before he was . . . the other two J's,": Matt Winkeljohn, "J Brothers, Always," *The Atlanta Journal-*

Constitution, Jan. 10, 2007, http://us.mg2.mail.yahoo.com/dc/launch?.rand=avq5k0inu277j, Nov. 24, 2008.

64   "I had been telling him . . . two more tries at the SAT: Carroll Rogers, "Way to Go, Joe," *The Atlanta Journal-Constitution*, Nov. 10, 1998, http://us.mg2.mail.yahoo.com/dc/launch?.rand=avq5k0inu277j, Nov. 24, 2008.

65   "Everybody thought I was crazy,": Barry Jacobs, "One of a Kind," *Georgia Tech: 2008-09 Basketball Media Guide*. p. 197, http://grfx.cstv.com/photos/schools/geot/sports/m-baskbl/auto_pdf/0809-m-baskbl-mg-9.pdf.

65   Some of what fans . . . bags over their heads.: Jacobs, p. 196.

65   "The ACC was just a great . . . lot of things to offer,": Jacobs, 197.

65   heavily favored to win the ACC title . . . stolen from Cremins.: Jacobs, p. 197.

65   "Not winning an ACC . . . almost ruined my life,": Jacobs, p. 197.

65   "That was the championship . . . pain away for me.": Jacobs, p. 198.

66   "I felt we deserved it,": Wilkinson, p. 135.

66   "That was our national championship right there.": Wilkinson, p. 137.

66   "Colorado had precedent . . . Tech's schedule and credentials.: Wilkinson, p. 137.

66   About four o'clock that afternoon, . . . UPI champs by one vote.: Wilkinson, p. 138.

66   "Justice was cone,": Wilkinson, p. 140.

67   Tech scored 32 touchdowns . . . after a Tech kickoff.: "Tech 222 Cumberland 0," *Georgia Tech Football: The Perfect Option: 2008 Media Guide*, p. 152, http://ramblinwreck.cstv.com/sports/m-football/spec-rel/08-fb-media-guide.html.

68   he had never played from a down stance,: John Hollis, "Means Justify Linebacker's Switch to End," *The Atlanta Journal-Constitution*," Dec. 31, 2003, http://us.mg2.mail.yahoo.com/dc/launch?.rand=avq5k0inu277j, Nov. 24, 2008.

68   But the Tech defensive line . . . quickness and overall athleticism.: Hollis.

68   "I did better than I . . . his stock with the pros,: Hollis.

69   During the warmups, Johnny McNeil . . . look at these guys?": Stinson, *Georgia Tech's Lethal Weapons*, p. 56.

69   "I don't know if they . . . only 41-40 at halftime.: Stinson, *Georgia Tech's Lethal Weapons*, p. 56.

69   The Jackets led eight . . . for 93 of the last 95 seconds,: Stinson, *Georgia Tech's Lethal Weapons*, p. 57.

69   Tech outrebounded LSU 52-51.: Stinson, *Georgia Tech's Lethal Weapons*, p. 57.

70   Roy Riegels "was sport's original goat.": Van Brimmer, *Stadium Stories*, p. 18.

70   When halfback Stumpy Thomason . . . Tech players tackled him.: Van Brimmer, *Stadium Stories*, p. 20.

70   Officials spotted the ball . . . punt in the second half.: Van Brimmer, *Stadium Stories*, p. 21.

71   "thought it was important to . . . could unite the alumni.": King, p. 59.

71   "Bill Curry was such a natural fit for Georgia Tech,": Akshay Amarane-

ni, "Bill Curry: 'A Class Act,'" *Technique*, Nov 21, 2008, http://www.nique.
net/nique/article/877, Jan. 17, 2009.

71   "It would be a rocky road until [Curry] got his program established.":
King, p. 59.

71   "Football attendance was down, . . . just as bad.": Amaraneni.

71   "We were bankrupt in . . . just to pay the bills.": Amaraneni.

72   "the quintessential goodwill ambassador for Georgia Tech,": Ballew, p.
33.

72   "Thirty-eight years I was . . . my whole life, really.": Ballew, pp. 33-34.

72   Five years later, he stopped . . . Dodd to hire Hyder.: Ballew, p. 31.

72   Once before a game against . . . for the second time that season.: Ballew,
pp. 31-32.

73   "one crossing light, a grocery store, and maybe two gas stations": Matt
Winkeljohn, "Georgia Tech Punter Releases the Hounds," *The Atlanta
Journal-Constitution*, Nov. 2, 2006, http://us.mg2.mail.yahoo.com/dc/
launch?.rand=avq5k0inu277j, Nov. 24, 2008.

73   "Blink, and you'll miss it," . . . hold on with your legs.": Winkeljohn,
"Georgia Tech Punter."

74   "a real gentleman . . . mentioning his golf game.": "Bobby Jones: Biography," http://www.bobbyjones.com/biography_scholarship.html, Nov. 19,
2008.

74   "the greatest amateur golfer ever.": "Bobby Jones (1902-1971)," *The New
Georgia Encyclopedia*, http://www.georgiaencyclopedia.org/nge/Article.
jsp?id=h-468, Nov. 19, 2008.

74   62 percent of the events he entered": Tom McCollister, "Bobby Jones –
Atlanta, Ga.," *2008 Georgia Tech Men's Golf*, p. 45, http://grfx.cstv.com/
photos/schools/geof/s;ports/m-golf/auto_pdf/history08.pdf.

74   "walked off the 11th . . . and into history,": McCollister.

74   "When Jones retired, . . . created another one." McCollister.

74   From the time he was 14 . . . than second ten times.: McCollister.

75   The great rivalry began at 3:15": Cormartie, p. 16.

75   "a stone was hurled . . . toward the boundary lines.": Cromartie, p. 19.

75   Since the freight was headed . . . arriving home after midnight.: Cromartie, p. 21.

76   That doggone Dodd Luck, you can't beat it.": Thomy, p. 153.

76   "Dodd's luck was really Dodd smart,": Van Brimmer, p. 36.

76   "Think you're lucky . . . waiting for something to happen.: Thomy, p.
152.

76   "During practice all week, . . . have to throw every down.": King, p. 24.

76   "Men, if we win . . . They're tight.": King, p. 24.

77   On the bus ride to . . . we're going to kick Clemson.": Wilkinson, p. 24.

77   the homecoming hors d'oeuvre. . . . to be a close game": Wilkinson, p.
24.

77   quarterback Shawn Jones and his . . . is ending right here,'": Wilkinson,
p. 22.

78   Most of the players were enrolled . . . assembled in time for
finals,: Ballew, p. 115.

78   I've always asked for . . . definitely believe in prayer.:

Bettinger, p. 95.

78   Bringing our need to God's love in faith is called prayer.: Culpepper, p. 239.

79   Chappell Rhino was a star on the . . . seldom used defensive back.: Van Brimmer, *Stadium Stories*, p. 78.

79   Offensive coordinator Frank Broyles . . . he could do it for me.": *Stadium Stories*, Van Brimmer, p. 80.

79   The Yellow Jacket nickname . . . in yellow coats and jackets.: "Tech Tradition," *Georgia Tech Football: The Perfect Option: 2008 Media Guide*, http://ramblinwreck.cstv.com/sports/m-football/spec-rel/08-fb-media-guide.html, p. 32.

80   King's high hopes were dampened . . . two hundred and fifth thousand dollars.": King, p. 54.

81   Defensive coordinator George O'Leary offered . . . O'Leary was.: Carroll Rogers, "A Home at Last," *The Atlanta Journal-Constitution*, Dec. 28, 1998, http://us.mg2.mail.yahoo.com/dc/launch?.rand=avq5k0inu277j, Nov. 24, 2008.

81   "a purely selfish matter . . . misfortune or frustration": Bruce T. Dahlberg, "Anger," *The Interpreter's Dictionary of the Bible* (Nashville: Abingdon Press, 1962), Vol. 1, p. 136.

82   "I really miss it," . . . from the Tech tower.: "Hook, Line & Sinker," *Georgia Tech: 2008-09 Basketball Media Guide*, p. 190, http://grfx.cstv.com/photos/schools/geot/sports/m-baskbl/auto_pdf/0809-m-baskbl-mg-9.pdf, Nov. 25, 2008.

83   "a disaster. Seems like nothing went right.": Thomy, p. 161.

83   Tech was winning easily . . . back with a broken nose,": Thomy, p. 161.

84   "a short-haired, square-jawed, real live bulldog.": Cromartie, p. 44.

84   "Tech's bulldog mascot became . . . for the first time.: Cromartie, p. 44.

84   Every summer in the 1950s, . . . before he left the station wagon.: Ballew, pp. 75-76.

85   were ranked 248th. . . . because of his experience.: Voisin.

85   He promised a national . . . within five years.: Wendy Parker, "Recruits from Far-Flung Hotbeds Lift Tech," *The Atlanta Journal-Constitution*, Dec. 8, 1996, http://us.mg2.mail.yahoo.com/dc/launch?.rand=avq5k0inu277j, Nov. 24, 2008.

86   who hoped to make the traveling squad.: Van Brimmer, *Stadium Stories*, p. 105.

86   Rodgers looked at him . . . put in Lanier or fold.'": Van Brimmer, *Stadium Stories*, p. 105.

86   "I should never had had . . . abilities out there.": Van Brimmer, *Stadium Stories*, p. 108.

86   when Lanier was sacked . . . "That's fine with me.": Van Brimmer, *Stadium Stories*, p. 102.

86   "Of all the quarterbacks who . . . Lanier laughed.: Van Brimmer, *Stadium Stories*, p. 112.

87   The term "Rambling Wreck" was first applied . . . donation of the car to The Institute.: "Tech," *Georgia Tech Track & Field: 2008*, http://ramblinwreck.cstv.com/sports/w-track/08-wtrack-media-guide.html, p. 50.

88   No soap and hot water. No pork or pastry. Bolton, *War Eagle*, p. 68.
88   inventing the shotgun snap. . . . distance before each play. Van Brimmer, *Stadium Stories*, p. 5.
88   He decreed that no two . . . punt anyway, anywhere.": Bolton, *War Eagle*, pp. 69-70.
88   175 axioms of play,: Van Brimmer, Stadium Stories, p. 9.
88   "Don't have your feet in the way . . . with your head up.": Bolton, p. 70.
88   He drew up twenty-one . . . stale or toasted bread.: Van Brimmer, *Stadium Stories*, p. 9.
89   she had to fight . . . spot on the squad.: Mike Knobler, "McDowell Wins Title in Singles, " *The Atlanta Journal-Constitution*, May 27, 2008, http://www.ajc.com/uga/content/printedition/2008/05/27/techtennis.html, Nov. 2, 2008.
89   "despicable, vile, unprincipled scoundrels.": John MacArthur, *Twelve Ordinary Men* (Nashville: W Publishing Group, 2002), p. 152.
90   "ankle deep in tears and sodas": Van Brimmer, *Stadium Stories*, pp. 130-31.
90   On the flight home, players and coaches danced in the aisles;: Van Brimmer, *Stadium Stories*, p. 131.
90   When he saw a roadblock . . . a fight or something.": Wilkinson, p. 90.
90   "Wall-to-wall people, . . . got their autographs.": Wilkinson, p. 90.
90   "bonfire of the insanities": Wilkinson, p. 91.
90   "It was as if we had just won the Super Bowl,": Van Brimmer, *Stadium Stories*, p. 132.
90   What are all these people doing?: Van Brimmer, *Stadium Stories*, p. 132.

BIBLIOGRAPHY

Aldinger, Charles. "Liberty Bowl 1972: Georgia Tech Iowa State." http://www.mm-bolding.com/bowls/Liberty_1972.htm.

Amaraneni, Akshay. "Bill Curry: 'A Class Act': A Look Back: Coaching in Tough Times (Head Coach 1980-1986)," *Technique*, Nov. 21, 2008, http://www.nique.net/nique/article/877.

Ballew, Bill. *Yellow Jackets Handbook: Stories, Stats and Stuff about Georgia Tech Basketball*. Wichita, KS: The Wichita Eagle and Beacon Publishing Co., 1996.

Barnhart, Tony. "The Final Four: Glow Spans Different Eras; Past Jackets Share in Success." *The Atlanta Journal-Constitution*. 1 April 2004. http://us.mg2.mail.yahoo.com/dc/launch?.rand=avq5k0inu277j.

Bettinger, Jim and Julie S. *The Book of Bowden*. Nashville: TowleHouse Publishing, 2001.

"Bobby Jones (1902-1971)." *The New Georgia Encyclopedia*. http://www.georgiaency-clopedia.org/nge/Article.jsp?id=h-468.

"Bobby Jones: Biography." http://www.bobbyjones.com/biography_scholarship.html.

Bolton, Clyde. *The Crimson Tide: A Story of Alabama Football*. Hunstville, AL: The Strode Publishers, 1972.

---. *War Eagle: A Story of Auburn Football*. Huntsville, AL: The Strode

Publishers, 1973.

Bradley, Mark. "Captain Sees His Old Ship Sail True." *The Atlanta Journal-Constitution*. 2 Dec. 2008. http://ww.ajc.com/sports/content/printedition/2008/12/02/bradley.html.

"Calvin Johnson (American Football)." *Wikipedia, the free encyclopedia*. http://en.wikipedia.org/wiki/Calvin_Johnson_(football).

Cromartie, Bill. *Clean Old-Fashioned Hate*. Huntsville, AL: The Strode Publishers, 1977.

Culpepper, R. Alan. "The Gospel of Luke: Introduction, Commentary, and Reflections." *The New Interpreter's Bible*. Vol. IX. Nashville: Abingdon Press, 1995. 1-490.

Dahlberg, Bruce T. "Anger." *The Interpreter's Dictionary of the Bible*. Vol. I. Nashville: Abingdon Press, 1962. 135-37.

Davidson, David. "NCAA Rushing Record." *Georgia Tech Football: The Perfect Option: 2008 Media Guide*. http://ramblinwreck.cstv.com/sports/m-football/spec-rel/08-fb-media-guide.html.

Davis, Katie B. "Pictures of the Past: From Birth to Earth: Billy Martin and Billy Lothridge Experienced Wins, and Most Importantly, Life During Their Careers." *The Gainesville Times*. July 9, 2008. http://www.gainesvilletimes.com/news/archive/6895.

Freeman, Criswell, ed. *The Wisdom of Southern Football*. Nashville: Walnut Grove Press, 1995.

Georgia Tech: 2008-09 Basketball Media Guide. http://grfx.cstv.com/photos/schools/geot/sports/m-baskbl/auto_pdf/0809-m-baskbl-mg-9.pdf.

"Georgia Tech Bands: Music Department History." http://gtband.net/joomla/index.php?option=com_content&task=view&id=65&Itemid=87.

"Georgia Tech Yellow Jacket Marching Band." *Wikipedia, the free encyclopedia*. http:///en.wikipedia.org/wiki/Georgia_Tech_Athletic_Bands.

"Georgia Tech Yellow Jackets Football: Home Stadium," *Wikipedia, the free encyclopedia*, http://en.wikipedia.org/wiki/Georgia_Tech_Yellow_Jackets_football.

Griffin, John Chander. *Georgia vs. Georgia Tech: Gridiron Grudge Since 1893*. Athens: Hill Street Press, 2000.

"Harping on Harpring." *Georgia Tech: 2008-09 Basketball Media Guide*. 191. http://grfx.cstv.com/photos/schools/geot/sports/m-baskbl/auto_pdf/0809-m-baskbl-mg-9.pdf.

Hartstein, Larry. "Chamblee High's Jones Runs Wild for Tech." *ajc.com*. http://www.ajc.com/sports/content/sports/gatech/stories/2008/11/29/georgia_tech_roddy.

Hiskey, Michelle. "A Cheerful Bequest: Family of Cheerleaders Uniquely Enriches Georgia Tech, Others' Lives." *The Atlanta Journal-Constitution*. 27 Feb. 2005. D1. http://us.mg2.mail.yahoo.com/dc/launch?.gx=1&rand=3rl2d803lim74.

Hollis, John. "Disease Can't Derail Desire." *The Atlanta Journal-Constitution*. 9 June 2004. E1. http://us.mg2.mail.yahoo.com/dc/launch?.gx=1&.rand=3rl2d803lim74.

---. "Means Justify Linebacker's Switch to End." *The Atlanta Journal-Constitution*. 31 Dec. 2003. http://us.mg2.mail.yahoo.com/dc/launch?.rand=avq5k0inu277j.

Holt, Andy. "Ramblin' with Chaunte Howard." *Technique*. 10 Sept. 2004. http://dev.nique.gatech.edu/issues/2004-09-10/sports.

"Hook, Line & Sinker." *Georgia Tech: 2008-09 Basketball Media Guide*. 190. http://grfx.
cstv.com/photos/schools/geot/sports/m-baskbl/auto_pdf/0809-m-baskbl-
mg-9.pdf.

Howard, Susan. "Taking It to the Hoop: Beneath His Playfulness, John Salley Has
a Driving Ambition." *The Atlanta Journal-Constitution*. 17 Nov. 1985. http://
us.mg2.mail.yahoo.com/dc/launch?.rand=avq5k0inu277j.

Jacobs, Barry. "One of a Kind." *Georgia Tech: 2008-09 Basketball Media Guide*. 196-99.
http://grfx.cstv.com/photos/schools/geot/sports/m-baskbl/auto_pdf/0809-m-
baskbl-mg-9.pdf.

King, Kim with Jack Wilkinson. *Kim King's Tales from the Georgia Tech Sideline*.
Champaign, IL: Sports Publishing L.L.C., 2004.

Knobler, Mike. "Dietitian Tips the Scales in Yellow Jackets' Favor." *The Atlanta
Journal-Constitution*. 8 Sept. 2006. http://us.mg2.mail.yahoo.com/dc/launch?.
rand=avq5k0inu277j.

---. "Excellence Required: Competitive Jackets Coach Paul Johnson Sets Tough
Standards for Himself and Others." *The Atlanta Journal-Constitution*. 16 Dec.
2007. http://us.mg2m.mail.yahoo.com/dc/launch?.rand=avq5k0inu277j.

---. "Jackets Duo Making Thievery Pay Off Big." *The Atlanta Journal-Constitution*. 22
March 2008. http://us.mg2.mail.yahoo.com/dc/launch?.rand=avq5k0inu277j.

---. "McDowell Wins Title in Singles." *The Atlanta Journal-Constitution*. 27 May
2008. http://www.ajc.com/uga/content/printedition/2008/05/27/techtennis.
html.

---. "Ready for Action: An Injury Kept Tech's Hodges out of Last Year's Regional."
The Atlanta Journal-Constitution. 3 June 2005. D1. http://us.mg2.mail.yahoo.
com/dc/launch?.gx=1&.rand=aj5tp61nsg1vj.

---. "Star Athletes Joe Hamilton, Brian Oliver Back at Ga. Tech to Finally Score
Diplomas." *The Atlanta Journal-Constitution*. 3 Aug. 2007. http://us.mg2.ya-
hoo.com/dc/launch?.rand=avq5k0inu277j.

Ledbetter, D. Orlando. "Jackets Rally Again to Win ACC Title." *The Atlanta Journal-
Constitution*. 30 May 2005. B1. http://us.mg2.mail.yahoo.com/dc/launch?.
gx=1&.rand=5jipv0jogmina.

Lomax, Patrice. "The Team That Bee-Lieved." *Georgia Tech: 2008-09 Basketball
Media Guide*. 174. http://grfx.cstv.com/photos/schools/geot/sports/m-baskbl/
auto_pdf/0809-m-baskbl-mg-9.pdf.

MacArthur, John. *Twelve Ordinary Men*. Nashville: W Publishing Group, 2002.

McCollister, Tom. "Bobby Jones – Atlanta, Ga." *2008 Georgia Tech Men's Golf*. 45.
http://grfx.cstv.com/photos/schools/geof/sprots/m-golf/auto_pdf/history08.
pdf.

Murphy. Austin. "Hands Down." *Sports Illustrated*. 23 Oct. 2006. http://vault.sports-
illustrated.cnn.com/vault/article/magazine/MAG1113320/index.htm.

Parker, Wendy. "Has Game, Will Travel (Quite Far): German Leads Tech to Honolulu." *The Atlanta Journal-Constitution*. 11 Dec. 2003. http://us.mg2.mail.
yahoo.com/dc/launch?.rand=avq5k0inu277j.

---. "Recruits from Far-Flung Hotbeds Lift Tech to National Prominence." *The Atlanta Journal-Constitution*. 8 Dec. 1996. http://us.mg2.mail.yahoo.com/
dc/launch?.rand=avq5k0inu277j.

"Retired Jersey #19: Clint Castleberry, RB." *Georgia Tech Football: The
Perfect Option: 2008 Media Guide*. 155. http://ramblinwreck.

cstv.com/sports/m-football/spec-rel/08-fb-media-guide.html.

Rogers, Carroll. "A Home at Last: Center Craig Page Finally Settled at Georgia Tech, Where He Became an All-American." *The Atlanta Journal-Constitution.* 28 Dec. 1998. http://us.mg2.mail.yahoo.com/dc/launch?.rand=avq5k0inu277j.

---. "Way to Go, Joe: Hurdling Obstacles Is Burns' Specialty." *The Atlanta Journal-Constitution.* 10 Nov. 1998. http://us.mg2.mail.yahoo.com/dc/launch?. rand=avq5k0inu277j.

Shamik, Morton and Robert Creamer. "A Rough Day for the Bear." *Sports Illustrated.* 26 Nov. 1962. http://vault.sportsillustrated.cnn.com/vault/article/magazine/MAG1074338/index.htm.

Stegeman, John E. *The Ghosts of Herty Field: Early Days on a Southern Gridiron.* Athens: The University of Georgia Press, 1997.

Stinson, Thomas M. "Georgia Tech Storms Past Georgia." *ajc.com.* http://www.ajc. com/sports/content/sports/gatech/stories/2008/11/29/tech_georgia_rivalry.

---. *Georgia Tech's Lethal Weapons: ACC Champs; 1990 Final Four.* Savannah: Golden Coast Publishing Company, 1990.

---. "The Start of Something Good." *Georgia Tech: 2008-09 Basketball Media Guide.* 188-89. http://grfx.cstv.com/photos/schools/geot/sports/m-baskbl/auto_pdf/0809-m-baskbl-mg-9.pdf.

Strickland, Carter. "Mitchell Outburst Rallies Jackets." *The Atlanta Journal-Constitution.* 17 March 2007. http://us.mg2m.mail.yahoo.com/dc/launch?. rand=avq5k0inu277j.

---. "Shelton's Jackets Climb to Top." *The Atlanta Journal-Constitution.* 23 May 2007. http://us.mg2m.mail.yahoo.com/dc/launch?.rand=avq5k0inu277j.

"Tech." *Georgia Tech Track & Field: 2008.* http://ramblinwreck.cstv/sports/w-track/08-wtrack-media-guide.html.

"Tech 222 Cumberland 0: Most Lopsided Game Ever Came in Atlanta in 1916." *Georgia Tech Football: The Perfect Option: 2008 Media Guide.* 152. http://ramblinwreck.cstv.com/sports/m-football/spec-rel/08-fb-media-guide.html.

"Tech Tradition: Rambling Wreck, Gold and White, Yellow Jacket Mascot." *Georgia Tech Football: The Perfect Option: 2008 Media Guide.* 32. http://ramblinwreck. cstv.com/sports/m-football/spec-rel/08-fb-media-guide.html.

Thomy, Al. *The Ramblin' Wreck: A Story of Georgia Tech Football.* Huntsville, AL: The Strode Publishers, 1973.

Van Brimmer, Adam. *Stadium Stories: Georgia Tech Yellow Jackets: Great Moments in Team History.* Guilford, CN: The Globe Pequot Press, 2006.

---. "Tech Heroes born in 'Drought' Years." *Augusta Chronicle.* 22 Nov. 2007. http://chronicle.augusta.com/stories/112207/gat_153435.shtml.

Voisin, Ailene. "Tech Stays on Road to Volleyball Elite." *The Atlanta Journal-Constitution.* 26 Sept. 1995. http://us.mg2.mail.yahoo.com/dc/launch?. rand=avq5k0inu277j.

Wilkinson, Jack. *Focused on the Top: Georgia Tech's Championship Story.* Atlanta: Longstreet Press, 1991.

Winkeljohn, Matt. "Built of Fire and Ice." *The Atlanta Journal-Constitution.* 9 May 2007. D1. http://us.mg2.mail.yahoo.com/dc/launch?.gx=1&. rand=3rl2d803lim74.

---. "Georgia Tech Punter Releases the Hounds." *The Atlanta Journal-Constitution.* 2 Nov. 2006. http://us.mg2.mail.yahoo.com/dc/launch?.rand=avq5k0inu277j.

---. "J Brothers, Always: Tech's Jeremis Smith Holds on to a Life Lost." *The Atlanta Journal-Constitution.* 10 Jan. 2007. http://us.mg2.mail.yahoo.com/dc/launch?.rand=avq5k0inu277j.

---. "Valuable Role Player Learning a New Role: McHenry Helps Out as Student Assistant." *The Atlanta Journal-Constitution.* 27 Dec. 2007. http://us.mg2.mail.yahoo.com/dc/launch?.rand=avq5k0inu277j.

INDEX
(LAST NAME, DEVOTION DAY NUMBER)